Mindset Dominance

Stop Self-Sabotage and Break Bad Habits

HELEN MITAS

First published by Busybird Publishing 2014

Copyright © 2014 Helen Mitas

Reprinted 2018

ISBN

Print: 978-1-925830-00-2

Ebook: 978-1-925260-02-1

Helen Mitas has asserted her right under the Copyright, Designs and Patents Act 1988 to be identified as the author of this work. The information in this book is based on the author's experiences and opinions. The publisher specifically disclaims responsibility for any adverse consequences, which may result from use of the information contained herein. Permission to use information has been sought by the author. Any breaches will be rectified in further editions of the book.

All rights reserved. No part of this publication may be reproduced, stored in or introduced into a retrieval system, or transmitted in any form, or by any means (electronic, mechanical, photocopying, recording or otherwise) without the prior written permission of the author. Any person who does any unauthorised act in relation to this publication may be liable to criminal prosecution and civil claims for damages. Enquiries should be made through the publisher.

Cover image by Busybird Publishing

Cover design by Busybird Publishing

Layout and typesetting: Busybird Publishing

Busybird Publishing
2/118 Para Road
Montmorency, Victoria
Australia 384
www.busybird.com.au

"Helen Mitas has written a brilliant book that any therapist would benefit from. I love the 'no BS' approach and the immensely practical, specific advice she gives. It's particularly suitable for business-type clients, particularly Alpha males and females who struggle to find time in their lives to work on themselves."
>	**Dr Steve Carey**
>	Director – Academy of Hypnotic Science

"I enjoyed reading your book. It is written in a very dynamic, flowing style. One does not get a chance to feel bored, uninterested or bogged down. It not only informs but entertains the reader and keeps us looking forward to what is to come.

"This 'forward looking movement', of course, goes beyond the bounds of the book itself, inspiring and hopefully motivating people into action.

"It is one thing to write a book filled with information and examples. It is another to write one that inspires us to want to really do something to engage with our own potential and open us up to real constructive change."
>	**Donald E. Treacher**
>	Counselling Psychologist & Psychotherapist – Founder of Human Relations for Every Day Living

"A big congrats to Helen Mitas. I just finished reading my autographed copy of *Mindset Dominance*. It is a great work, Helen, and a credit to you. Not the usual *yada yada yada* and I would suggest an essential read and tool for anybody in the hypnotherapy and helping fields, or for those looking to gain the most from themselves."
>	**Rick Collingwood**
>	Director – Australian Academy of Hypnosis

I dedicate this book to Jon Bartholomeusz, my twin flame for 22 years of my life.

Jon - I thank you from the deepest part of my heart for the love and support that you gave me during our time together; where I experienced so much joy and so many blessings.

This book would not have been possible without you.

Thank You

Special Thanks

I would like to thank, in no particular order, the following people who have helped me manifest my goals, dreams and aspirations:

Special thanks to my son, Peter, who knows exactly the right moment when his mum is in need of a hug and a strong dose of love. You are a shining light, my gorgeous boy. I am so very proud of the mature, intelligent, kind man that you now are. You are forever challenging me to think differently.

My parents, Stratis and Christalla, for giving me the world's best family and who taught us all to love and forgive unconditionally.

My wise and loving siblings, John, Kathy, Doris, and Christine, brothers-in-law, sisters-in-law, nephews and nieces – I adore each and every one of you.

Special thanks to my eldest nephew – the ultimate fit executive – Andrew Michaels for his inspiration, candid interview, and photos.

Don Treacher, who was the first person who showed me the light and literally changed my life. I can never, ever thank you enough for all that you did for me.

Love and gratitude to my friend and confidante, Anna McDowall, who is always there to listen to me and support me. Everyone needs an Anna in their life!

My beautiful friends Brett Sinclair, Chris, Felicia, Glen, and Esmeralda who have stayed the distance through life's adversities and fill my soul with love.

Thank you to Natasa Denman for being a constant source of inspiration to me.

My clients, who have entrusted me to guide them through a tiny part of life's challenges and adversities as others have guided me when I needed a helping hand.

Contents

Special Thanks		i
About Helen		1
Introduction		3
1	Response Ability	15
2	Beyond Labels	31
3	Subconscious Creations	43
4	False Perceptions	59
5	Eureka Moments	69
6	It's Just BS	81
7	Balancing Act	95
8	Target Practice	105
9	Eat Like You Mean It	119
10	Booze Buster	131
11	Non-negotiables	143
12	Forever Fit	159
13	Andrew's Interview	171
This is the Beginning – A Conclusion -		179

About Helen

Helen Mitas is the founder of the world's first global Hypnotherapy clinic, Hypnofit® with 14 Hypnotherapy clinics in Australia, New Zealand ,U.S.A and the United Kingdom. The ethos of Hypnofit® is about providing a holistic solution from an emotional, mental and physical perspective. It's about recognising that how we think, affects how we feel and behave.

Mindset Dominance unpacks how we think and feel at the subconscious level so that we can change our actions with conscious intention, without subconscious patterns and programs getting in the way.

At the age of 28, Helen went through the most challenging time of her life, which led to Depression and Chronic Anxiety.

Helen slowly and systematically changed every area of her life, stepping into empowerment and self belief.

Helen let go of her limiting beliefs , lost 14 kilos and became fitter in her 40s than she ever was in her 20s. Helen competed in running events, winning medals and achieving what she once considered to be unachievable.

Helen let go of her corporate role and all the security it offered to follow her life's passion.

Helen has presented and trained therapists in the HypnoFit® Success System across the globe from New York to London. There are over 3,000 Hypnotherapists from over 20 countries who are now Certified HypnoFit® Therapists & Partners.

In her 53rd year, Helen decided to reclaim her birth name Eleni, as she realised that these achievements meant nothing, and the essence of her soul meant everything.

Eleni has an unwavering determination to remind you of your divine gift, and to help you get out of your own way to share your mission with the world.

SCAN ME

Introduction

"Even for the neurotic executive – as for everyone else – work has great therapeutic value; it is generally his last refuge, and deterioration there marks the final collapse of the man; his marriage, his social life, and the outside interests – all have suffered beforehand."

Richard A Smith

I know who you are. You have done whatever it takes to be successful in your life. You have sacrificed. You have worked long hours.

During this process of sacrificing, achieving and succeeding in your life, you have forgotten about the most important part: your health.

Now you are left with an unflattering belly. You are left with clothes that are way too tight for you. You feel embarrassed. People perceive you as being confident, but that cannot be further from the truth.

You have become unhealthy and you are wondering how you are going to enjoy the rest of your life when you feel so unfit. How are you going to reap the benefit of all the sacrifices that you have made up to this point?

The intention of this book is to help you take control so that you can feel as confident and as successful as you really are – to look as kick-ass on the outside as you are on the inside!

The clients who come to my Hypnotherapy clinic are struggling with their weight. They usually come because they want to lose weight, reduce their alcohol intake, or both.

The problem is usually their perception of time and how this affects the amount of exercise they do and their choices in relation to food and alcohol.

Their poor choices are usually attributed to being time-poor and the circumstances that they find themselves in. This book will show you how to manage the areas of your life that you have previously neglected to a standard that will get you the outcomes you want with maximum effect and minimum effort.

It is time to make some conscious choices about discovering the real reasons as to why this situation has developed and what needs to change. You want to

Introduction

be free to move forward into a compelling future where you will be fit and healthy and able to enjoy all the successes that you deserve.

I worked in the corporate sector for over 22 years in the areas of Credit Management, Information Technology and Energy Sector Regulation. I also worked as a Senior Policy Analyst, Senior Project Manager and Consultant for various large companies, and was responsible for the implementation of domestic and international projects. During this time, I found that I was spending so much time and effort in the workplace doing whatever it took to climb the corporate ladder, my health and personal wellbeing was slowly deteriorating.

This understanding came to me one day when I realised that every time I planned leave, I would instantly get sick. My body was accustomed to operating on adrenaline to get through the workday. My adrenal and immune systems were being stressed out and operating at critically low levels. So, the moment I took a break, there was nothing left in the "tank" to keep me going.

I was carrying extra weight. I became more unfit and, year after year, it was becoming harder and harder to do anything about it. When I finally decided that my health was an absolute priority and that, no matter what, I was going to lose the extra weight I was carrying, my life changed. The remarkable aspect of this transformation is that my success in the workplace was not adversely impacted when I began to focus on my health.

In fact, the reverse occurred. I became even more successful in my work than I had ever been before. As I became physically stronger and healthier, I also became more emotionally and mentally fit. I was naturally happier. My success in the workplace reflected my physical, mental, and emotional transformation.

My passion is to share all the wonderful lessons I learnt throughout my journey of becoming strong and fit. I want to help you remove the limiting beliefs and blocks that are holding you back from moving forward in your life. I want to help propel you towards a compelling future where you can have it all, the same way I did.

When I first started my physical transformation, it was all about losing weight. I discovered that the more I exercised, the more I could eat, because I LOVED my food. Food was always very important in my family.

So, I started this regime of exercising intensely for the sole reason of being able to eat more.

I conscientiously counted the kilojoules and fat content of every item I ate, documented and graphed my progress.

I discovered the point where I could exercise and eat the amount of food I wanted to eat without feeling deprived and still lose weight.

The key was discipline without deprivation.

Introduction

It was important for me not to get back on that diet rollercoaster that I had been on as a teenager and young adult. It was important that I did not feel like I was deprived or on a diet. It was about making smarter food choices whilst exercising at the same time.

Exercise became a non-negotiable activity for me.

As I started to exercise, it became more than just a means of containing my calorie input. I found myself getting stronger. I found myself breaking through barriers and limitations that I had previously placed upon myself. When I started to run, it was a massive breakthrough for me, because up to that point I had always imagined that running was for other people. I would see fun runs on the TV and I perceived that "running world" to be a parallel universe, which I did not understand or belong in.

One night, I signed up at a new gym. I was asked the standard questions and the conversation with my new Personal Trainer went something like this:

Personal Trainer:	"What exercise do you do?"
Me:	"I walk."
Personal Trainer:	"Have you considered running?"
Me:	"I don't run."
Personal Trainer:	"Why not?"

I considered this question for a moment and responded with what seems now to be a ridiculous answer, **"Because I don't run!"**

The thought of running had NEVER crossed my mind. Me? A runner? No way!

The Personal Trainer suggested a strategy that I call **pole to pole**.

It is simple and goes like this: Start walking ... pick a light-pole and jog to it ... continue walking ... pick another pole and jog to it ... walk to the next pole and run to the next one, and so on. It was not too long before I could run further and faster.

I then became one of those people from that "parallel universe" who participated in fun runs and running competitions! I never have imagined this was possible for me!

At this stage, I knew that I could do anything – provided I focused on it.

I started to lift weights. I was getting stronger, and it felt so good to feel strong.

Introduction

I am proud that I am strong and fit and that I am a person who exercises *no matter what*. Moving my body to a high level of intensity every day has become my priority.

Prior to my life of consistent exercise, I used to feel lethargic and at times sad for no apparent reason. Even now, if for some reason I do not exercise because I am struck down by injury or something of that nature, I feel that I need to make the effort to keep myself upbeat.

When this happens, and I do not exercise, I feel the effects for the entire day. I feel low, lethargic, exhausted, and tired. The thought that inevitably enters my mind is, "Is this the way the other half live? Do people choose not to move their body and start the day feeling like this every single day?"

The chapters of this book will take you through the same step-by-step transformation in your thinking and your wellbeing.

It all started when I made some big realisations about what was holding me back at the subconscious level and what needed to happen for me to break through. I developed my own very powerful strategies so that I could move forward.

By becoming aware of what was holding me back subconsciously and by eliminating my limiting beliefs, I was able to surge forward to a future where I was physically healthier in my 40s than I ever was in my 20s. During this journey, I discovered some very powerful strategies that worked for me and eventually for thousands of my clients. This book is about sharing those strategies with you.

Chapter 1 reflects that, initially, it was all about stepping up and taking **responsibility** for *everything* going on in my life. It was about getting out of victim mode and taking on a winning mindset where I decided that I am responsible and in control of my thoughts, feelings, actions, and consequently, my life.

Chapter 2 reflects the next stage, which was about the need to let go of any labels and beliefs that I had identified with, which were holding me back such as: being 'too old', 'not the kind of person who runs', 'not a morning person', etc. The belief that I would never run just because I had never run before was eliminated. The belief that I was too old to lift weights because I was in my late 30s was eliminated. I let go of all those labels and beliefs that held me back from achieving everything that I wanted to achieve.

Chapter 3 explains the process of discovering what your subconscious strategies are that keep you stuck . As soon as you discover your unhelpful subconscious strategies , you are then able to bring them into your conscious awareness and do something about them.

Chapter 4 is about false perceptions and understanding that your perception of life is a filtering system that is unique to you. This chapter helps you take control of your emotions enabling you to become a more balanced and contented person where you are less likely to resort to addictive behaviour such as overeating or drinking excessive alcohol.

Introduction

When you understand that the way you perceive the events in your life is based on your own filtering system and can then see these events objectively from another person's point of view, you are then in control of your emotions.

When we attain the skill of looking at our life objectively, we have the clarity to discover what is happening underneath the surface. Chapter 5 explores what is at the very core of why we do things. What is it that we really need? What are we hungry for in life? What is it that we are lacking? What can we do to get there?

Chapter 6 redefines the reasons people give themselves for not taking action and suggests that most of the reasons we have for not achieving our goals to date, are purely and simply **BS**. You didn't have to choose between working hard or exercising hard. You can be effective in every area of your life by being honest and removing the BS reasons that stop you from becoming the person you have the potential to be.

In Chapter 7 we discover the *balancing act*, where our actions, thoughts and feelings are aligned to what we feel is important in life. Whatever it is that we hold dear in our hearts, whatever it is that we emotionally connect with, that is where our focus and attention needs to be. Step-by-step, we get closer to achieving our goals, as we now have the empowering beliefs and strategies to live a kick-ass life.

Becoming very clear and focused on what you really want in life is what Chapter 8 is all about. We can spend so much of our lives obsessing about what we don't want, that our real goals are not even in our conscious minds. **Take aim and fire**!

Chapters 9 and 10 are full of practical strategies that you can use when attending conventions, conferences and Friday night drinks so that you are making smarter choices with **food and alcohol**, without feeling like you are deprived or on a diet.

Then you are ready in Chapter 11 to raise the bar and create some high standards about what the **'non-negotiables'** will now be in your new, empowered life. By being consistent with your high standards and your non-negotiables, you will achieve your goals. It is inconsistency that pulls you away from your goals.

Chapter 12 is all about making sure that your new **habits stick** and stay with you for the long haul.

Finally, in chapter 13, there is a bonus interview with someone I consider to be the **ultimate kick-ass executive**. My eldest nephew, Andrew is a marketing professional in the corporate world. His winning mindset on health and fitness helps him to have it all.

His work involves a lot of travel with multiple challenges, and yet he manages to maintain a healthy, strong body at optimal fitness. He has managed to strike an amazing balance between his personal and his work goals, so that he excels in every area of his life. Andrew shares his secrets with me as he responds to specific questions about the strategies he lives his life by.

All you need to do is implement the changes suggested at the rate of one chapter per week, and within 90 days you will have a complete transformation which will be long-lasting.

Introduction

Congratulations for deciding to make some kick-ass changes in your life to make the most of your one shot at life – after all, we only get one!

1

Response Ability

"The price of greatness is responsibility."
Winston Churchill

This chapter is not about how you balance your various responsibilities; it is about getting to first base, which entails taking responsibility for everything that's going on in your life.

You will need to take responsibility for what has happened in your past, for what is happening right now, and for what you want in your future.

Only when you can accept total responsibility will you have the ability to take control.

When clients first come to me wanting to make some changes in their life, the first question I ask them is:

"Are you ready to make a change now?"

Once they answer, "Yes", I ask them:

"Who is responsible for making that change?"

Most of them will answer, "I am", but a small percentage will say, "Perhaps you have got some responsibility here, too – after all, isn't that what I'm paying you for?"

My response is always the same.

"I can give you all the tools, strategies, and guidelines that you need, but I can't make you take action; only you can do that."

I am not going to be there forcing them out the door to go for their morning walk. People must take action on their own. When they can accept that challenge, I ask them to what percentage they are responsible for making the changes they want in life.

100% is the only answer!

Once they say that they are 100% responsible for the changes in their life, we are ready to get started.

1   Response Ability

Once you have accepted 100% responsibility for making changes in your life, then you can focus your attention on what needs to change. When you are ready to change the direction of your life and take action, you will inevitably get a different outcome.

It could be that you have attained success in your work life, but this success has not yet manifested itself in your personal life. If this is the case, you need to focus on your personal goals so that they can be aligned with your successful work life.

What is Responsibility?

Responsibility is the ability to respond. Do you have the ability to respond to the direction your life is taking?

Responsibility is where we take 100% ownership for every experience in our life. We need to be very clear that responsibility does not mean that we are at fault.

Responsibility does not equal Fault

For example, if you are a victim of crime, you are not at fault – you did not commit the crime, but you are responsible for the way that you react to that event and how that event will affect your life moving forward.

Another example would be if your marriage is not going the way you expected it would and your perception is that you are not at fault. It could be that your partner has done something that has broken your trust or contravened one of your marital agreements. It may have even been a "deal breaker". Even if your perception is that you are not at fault, you must take responsibility for your role in the relationship and do everything in your power to rectify the situation – if that's what you want.

Cause versus Effect

Do you operate out of "cause" or "effect"?

Do you take control of the direction in your life or are you a victim of circumstance?

To demonstrate this point clearly, I would like you to have a look at the Cause and Effect Model diagram (on the opposite page) where the vertical axis relates to the level of responsibility and the horizontal axis relates to whether the event is positive or negative.

This diagram is particularly useful to map how you perceive your role in life events. It is possible to swing between the various quadrants depicted below but we tend to either stay "above" (at "cause") or "below" (at "effect") the negative or positive axis shown in the diagram.

The diagram can be used to map how you are reacting to an event and whether you are operating at "cause" or at "effect" in your life.

Helen's Cause & Effect Model

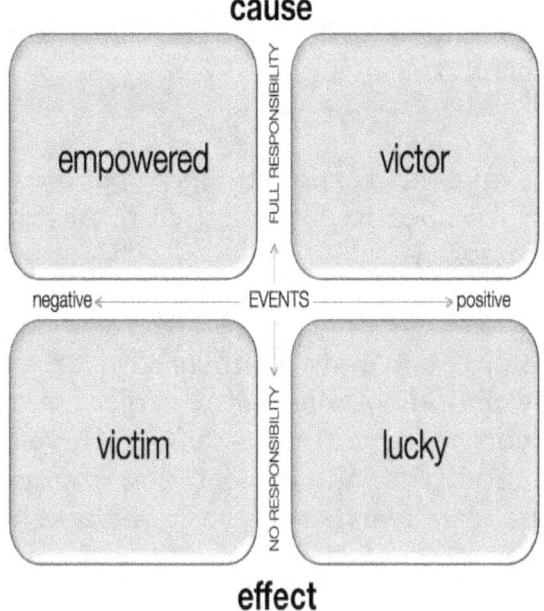

Look at the bottom right hand quadrant. If you take no responsibility but something positive happens (for instance, you get a pay rise), then you may think of yourself as "lucky".

So, if you perceive that the situation is out of your control, you are operating at "effect", not cause", even when the event is positive.

If you move to the bottom left hand quadrant, where something negative happens but you still take no responsibility – for instance, a job redundancy – then you are a victim of circumstance. This is where you perceive that "bad" things happen to you. So many people operate from this quadrant. It is the "poor me" syndrome. As you are operating at the bottom of the horizontal line in the diagram below, you are operating at "effect".

If you choose not to take any responsibility – if you have decided that your boss or the economy was to blame for your job redundancy – then you have not learned anything at all and you are likely to repeat the same patterns over again.

When you take no responsibility, you are operating at "effect", irrespective of whether the event itself is positive or negative.

For example, if you have sponsored a project that is not doing well and you blame the project manager and the team, you are operating at "effect". If you can take full responsibility for the project, you are operating at "cause" and can learn from your mistakes and find out what you need to do differently next time.

If you are having a discussion with your work colleagues and they do not understand your point, you need to take 100% responsibility for the fact that your meaning is not understood. You need to take a different approach so that you are communicating effectively. It is your responsibility, not theirs, to make sure that they understand you. You cannot blame them for not understanding you if you are not being clear in your communications.

When you embrace this presupposition, you commit to the response and ask for feedback to clarify your communication. It is all up to you. When it is all up to you, you can change and improve your situation. When you accept total responsibility, you are operating at "cause", and this is an empowering place to operate from.

The important principle to understand is that it does not matter whether the event is positive or negative – what matters is your reaction to the event. Your reaction determines whether you are operating from an empowered position (i.e. at cause) or a disempowered position (i.e. at effect).

A Tall Order – Sandra

Sandra was a client of mine who came to me for help with depression. She was a Head Chef who found herself in untenable situations at every restaurant she worked in, where she felt compelled to leave once issues came to a head. She couldn't understand why she was treated like this because she was an excellent Chef and received excellent feedback from customers.

She was also super-organised and effectively managed the restaurants in the owners' absence. Despite this, once she resigned, she wasn't given farewell lunches like the workers who had left before her and no one tried to talk her out of leaving. When Sandra came to me, she felt that she was treated poorly everywhere she went and she took no responsibility for the way her employment ceased at every place she worked.

If Sandra had taken responsibility and closely examined her own behaviour, she would have found that all these results were because she took it upon herself to be in control of all the areas of the restaurant, including the Front of the House, not just the kitchen. The Front of House Managers felt as though they were being micro-managed by an over-controlling Chef and the owner had to deal with dissatisfied staff.

When Sandra took responsibility for the friction in her workplace, she was able to change her style and be more flexible in working with other people.

When you are operating above the line (Cause and Effect Model), then you are operating at "cause", as you take responsibility for everything that happens in your life. In the top left-hand corner of the diagram, even when the event is negative, if you are taking full responsibility, then you are empowered to make the changes that you need to make.

Learn from your experiences and move on

The important thing to note is that, where total responsibility is taken, it does not matter whether the event is positive or negative. In this example, Sandra is empowered when she learns from the experience, makes the changes needed, and moves forward.

In Sandra's situation, the result is still negative, as she no longer has a job – but, because she has now taken full responsibility, she is empowered to move forward with the experience and knowledge needed to avoid making the same mistakes in the future.

The following questions can provide insights into your role in how the events played out around you.

Critical Questions to Ask Yourself
"What value do I add to the people around me?"

1 Response Ability

"Am I communicating my worth?"

"How could I have gotten a different response?"

"What would have had to have happened to have had a better outcome?"

"What is it that I did or didn't do?"

When you become empowered, you can make the necessary changes, so you won't repeat the same mistakes.

However, those who refuse to recognise and take responsibility for their role in the event will blame everyone but themselves and will have learned nothing. These people are going to continue to repeat the same mistakes until they can take responsibility for their role in the circumstances presented to them.

The top right-hand quadrant of the Cause and Effect Model is where full responsibility is taken. When you take responsibility, you are at "cause" in your life, not at 'effect'. Irrespective of whether the event is positive or negative, when you are at "cause", you are in control. It is a wonderful place to be in.

When a positive event does happen and you take full responsibility, then you can reap the benefits of your successes and be very proud of what you have achieved, giving yourself credit for your role in the success.

"In the long run, we shape our lives, and we shape ourselves. The process never ends until we die. And the choices we make are ultimately our own responsibility."

Eleanor Roosevelt

Bursting at the Seams – James

James, a successful businessman, came to see me to help him lose some excess kilos. James had recently married, and he was embarrassed by the way that he looked to his much younger wife. When he first came to see me, his shirts were popping open!

As a leader in his industry, he would stand up in front of his peers to deliver many keynote speeches and felt embarrassed because the buttons on his shirt were ready to burst.

He told me that he was committed to change and he paid up front for a program so that he could lose the weight he needed and get rid of his destructive habits.

He only lasted three sessions. Three sessions are not enough to make the permanent changes required for deeply embedded habits. I've seen this again and again with clients who are very busy. These clients are not prepared to see things through to the end, even though they appeared committed in the beginning.

The cost of putting your business goals ahead of your health is great: Illness, disability or death. Do you want to pay that price?

The Sickness Equation
Business Goals > Health Goals = Sickness

It is absolutely critical that you take responsibility for your long-term health.

This is the most important thing that you have to do in your life.

You cannot make a half-hearted or spur-of-the-moment commitment to changing your health and then set it aside or put it on the backburner when something "more important" comes up. You must make a commitment and dedicate yourself to the outcome. Your life could depend on it!

The problem is, people do not realise that their health is the most valuable asset they have until it has been compromised. Unless you assign your health the value it deserves, the most likely scenario is that its value will hit you in the face when you are in hospital or you can't return to work because you are ill.

How Our Society Views Responsibility

The use of antidepressants has doubled in Australia over the last decade (Trends in the utilisation of psychotropic medication in Australia from 2000 to 2011 – Stephenson, Karanges & McGregor). This shows that we are increasingly placing control into external forces such as drug companies, rather than our own internal resources.

Paxil and Zoloft are two of the most popular anti-anxiety medications and are ranked 7th and 8th respectively in the top 10 prescribed medications in the United States.

What we can infer from these statistics is that people are placing responsibility outside themselves. They want a quick solution to their medical conditions, and the drug companies are very happy to provide that solution for them.

You need to make these vital decisions now and stick to them. You need to schedule time in your calendar, so you can take consistent action. Change is not going to happen in a matter of weeks; it takes months for change to happen. It takes several months to turn actions into habits. It is your responsibility to see this through to the end. Do not be one of those overweight and unhealthy people that gives up and loses focus, getting distracted by seemingly more important tasks. They are not more important. What you are doing right now is the most important thing that you will ever do.

How Can I be Responsible for Everything?
People will often ask, "How can I be responsible for everything? Surely there are some things that I can't be responsible for. What about if a crime is conducted by some other person? How can I be responsible for that?"

"What if an employee was dishonest and stole from your company?"

"What if you're unfairly treated by your manager?"

1 Response Ability

"What if you're in an accident that wasn't your fault?"

You can be responsible in all these examples because you have complete control of your reaction to that event.

When Nelson Mandela was unjustly imprisoned for twenty-seven years, he stated that he did not suffer, but he prepared. He prepared for the day his country would be liberated. Whether he lived or died in prison, he said his country would be liberated from apartheid and he took responsibility for the way he thought and felt for the whole twenty-seven years he was in that prison cell.

Your action is to take responsibility

You need to get a medical health check right now and take full responsibility for your health.

Your workload is not responsible for your big belly.

Your over-demanding boss is not responsible for the fact that your shirt buttons are ready to pop open.

No one is responsible for you except you! If you do not take care of your health, no one else will. Self-care is one of the most important things you can do for yourself, your family, your staff, and your business.

You are responsible

Accept this as fact and make a commitment to do something about it.

No More Beer Belly – Jason

I have an example of someone who has succeeded diligently with everything that I had set out for him. This particular person – we will call him Jason – is a CEO of a large company. When he first came to me, it was for the sole purpose of reducing his alcohol intake because he believed it was out of control.

Jason knew he was drinking too much and it was having a negative effect. He also knew he could not sustain this habit. Jason committed to a program with me and he was diligent from the beginning. He left his ego at the door; he came in prepared to accept direction. He took responsibility by making sure that he turned up to every single session and diligently completed the tasks that I set for him in between sessions. He has reaped the benefits and the success has been amazing!

Apart from reducing his alcohol intake significantly, we have also achieved much more. He has lost his beer belly (even though he did not drink beer – he drank wine!), he is now doing more exercise than he has done for a very long time and has become very fit.

It is just wonderful to see that he came to me for one reason, and that was alcohol moderation, but by the end of the program he had achieved so much more by losing weight and getting fit by exercising. Now we are working on improving his relationship with his wife and bringing passion back into his marriage.

What We Can Get From These Examples

You can see how James wasted his time and money on a program that he paid for up front yet only attended three sessions, did not do any of the homework, and then quit. He reverted to old habits of making the wrong choices in terms of what should have been most important in his life – his health.

Jason, on the other hand, committed to the program, attended every session, and completed any task that I gave to him. As a result, we achieved so much more than the original scope of what we set out to do. That was because he was committed and took responsibility.

He was not too proud to complete the tasks at home. He recognised that I am the expert on this subject matter and did whatever was required.

It was because he did whatever it took that he is in a much happier, healthier place than he has been for many years. He has become healthy, fit and energised.

So, the important thing to remember is that, regardless of whether the event is negative or positive, your positive reaction helps you become empowered and be in control.

Power Points – Chapter 1
1. In order to achieve total control over our lives, we need to accept total responsibility for our choices, life's direction, and the resulting outcomes.

2. We need to focus on our personal goals as well as our work-related goals to be successful in our personal life and our work life.

3. Taking responsibility keeps us out of victim mode.

4. We need to own our problems; by owning our problems, we also own our successes.

MD ACTION 1

Get a thorough medical check-up and address the issues that may arise.

2

Beyond Labels

"My feeling is that labels are for canned food. I am what I am – and I know what I am."

Michael Stipe

If you have taken responsibility for everything going on in your life and you are ready for change, the very next step is to get rid of all the labels that are holding you back.

Labels are given to us by society, but we also willingly take them. These labels limit us in what we can accomplish. We must free ourselves from all labels and move past those definitions that have defined us. This removes any limits on what we can achieve.

Become flexible in your view of what you are capable of. Your flexibility will hold you in good stead when changes happen. Change is going to happen whether you like it or not. It is inevitable.

If you are flexible, if you can adapt to change, then you can remain in control

The more flexible your thinking is, the more you can adapt and succeed in an ever-changing world. If you are not flexible and stay stuck in the way that you currently do things, nothing will ever change.

If you remind yourself that you are more than just your label, then you have the opportunity to be passionate about all the different aspects of your life. You can bring that energy into your work life as well.

For the past thirty years, the prevalence of obesity in Australians has been steadily increasing. From 2011–2012, around 60% of Australian adults were labelled as overweight or obese. Does this label hold them back from being everything that they could possibly be?

If you identify yourself as fat, you will think, feel, and behave like a fat person. If you identify yourself as a lazy person, you will think, feel, and behave in a lazy way. If you identify yourself as a depressed person, you will feel depressed. Your belief system becomes your reality.

Removing these labels from your identity will open you up to everything that is possible for you.

The Occupation Label

Labels such as "The Provider", "The Successful Businessperson", "The CEO", "The Private Secretary" and "The Marketing Manager" are occupational labels. They do not help you become successful in all areas of your life. They only help you feel successful in that area of your life defined by the label.

In today's society, we have become our job titles. We often define ourselves by those titles. When we do this, we limit how we think, feel, and behave. Being more than a label allows you to be more than a person who holds a specific position.

Thinking outside this box broadens your horizons and increases your options. It opens up the possibilities of what you can do. If you can see yourself as more than your job title, you can be anything you want! What about a most incredible, awesome dad, a healthy role model for your children, or a sexy partner to your spouse? Any of these can become compelling reasons for making major changes in your life.

Who are you at your very core? Get in touch with the person beneath that position and status label. Are you a son? Are you a daughter? Grandson? Granddaughter? Husband? Wife? Are you a poet? A runner? Who are you really? How much time do you spend nurturing these other parts of you?

I do not believe that you are defined by the job that you do. I truly believe that there is so much more to you than your job. The work is what you do most of the time but it is not *who you are.*

I find it so interesting that when travelling through Europe, wherever you go, nobody ever asks what you do. Nobody cares! It is considered irrelevant. Nobody ever asked me what my occupation was – and I mean no one! You are more than your job. Europeans are far more interested in your opinion on various life issues than they are in your job status. In general, Europeans consider that your views define you as a person, not what you do during the day.

I can hear you asking, "What if you're happy with your job and you want to be defined by your title?" I am not suggesting you distance yourself from your job title; I am suggesting you start to see yourself as more than that. Start seeing yourself in all the various roles you have had in your life. Start seeing yourself beyond your job and for who you really are.

The Fat and Lazy Label
If you think the "fat and lazy" label describes you, you are going to identify as a fat and lazy person. This label will define your thoughts and actions, and your behaviours will reflect that identity.

Just because you find it hard to wake up in the morning does NOT mean that you are not a morning person. It just means that you have not yet found a strategy to get out of bed early with the right motivation and attitude.

The past does not define you either.

Just because you have never been to the gym in the past does not mean you cannot go in the future. The past does not equal the future. This is now! You just need to find a strategy that works for you.

The Emotion Label

Just because you are stressed at this point in your life does not mean you are a stressed person. Just because you are anxious does not mean you are an anxious person. It just means you are not finding empowering ways to remain calm and peaceful.

If you identify yourself as a depressed person, you will feel depressed. Your belief system becomes your reality so, get rid of those labels. Whatever you are feeling at the time is not who you really are. It is just what you are feeling in this moment. The next moment is up to you.

The Depression Label

There are many people who have been diagnosed with depression and they feel that it restricts them from ever being motivated or being able to move forward. When clients first come to see me and inform me that they have been diagnosed with depression, they believe that they have an illness that they will need to endure for the rest of their lives.

Depression is a label we give to people who have a depressed mood most of the time, that have lost interest or pleasure in most activities, are fatigued, cannot sleep, feel hopeless and helpless, cannot think clearly, or cannot make decisions. That label tells us nothing about the cause of those symptoms.

A diagnosis of clinical depression is based on a set of symptoms. There is no blood test that tells you that you are depressed. There is no gene that tells you that you are depressed. That is right – there is no depression gene! These same symptoms can be applicable to a number of 'disorders'. The patient's fate is left in the hands of the medical practitioner who has chosen the disorder he or she thinks is most applicable to their patient and, *voila,* a diagnosis is made!

The patient will walk away from the appointment feeling disempowered, with their goals, dreams or aspirations seemingly beyond their grasp.

I am not saying that depression does not exist. Of course it does. What I am saying is that the depression *label* will hold you back from everything that you can be. You are more than that, are you not?

It is possible to live an empowered life and acknowledge that, although you are feeling depressed, life is not out of your control. Depression can be managed and eliminated.

You need to find a therapist who will support you to find the root cause of your problems and who can help you to eliminate them and live an empowered life.

The Age Label
And then there is the "age" label. Many people believe that they are too old to do something different.

Although your age may slow you down, it will not prevent you from living your life to its full potential.

You do have the ability to be the best that you can possibly be. There is no doubt about that. You need to remove that "age" label.

Get rid of those labels: the age label, the occupation label, and the emotion label. They only hold you back..

Get rid of them!

> *"I don't like labels. I think they conceal more than they reveal, sort of like a bikini."*
>
> **Arlen Specter**

Guilty of Being a Home Maker – Kirsty

One of my clients, Kirsty, is the owner of a legal firm and was significantly overweight when she first came to me for weight loss. Kirsty is also a Barrister, so she needed to attend court on a regular basis to represent her clients. She told me that she felt embarrassed with the way that she looked, especially as she had to stand up in court and articulate her cases. She had to appear confident, yet she felt like a slob.

She would be standing there in her high heels, but she felt like she was carrying way too much weight. She felt unsteady and lacked confidence in the way she presented herself.

Kirsty was overweight because she engaged in "reward eating". In other words, she ate to reward herself rather than as a form of required energy.

Kirsty's adult children and husband expected her to manage all the demands of the household as well as a high-pressure legal career. She would come home from work feeling exhausted and it was still expected that she would get dinner ready for a house full of adults. The home duties were hers simply because she was the wife and mother.

Kirsty created this millstone around her own neck. She never asked her children to help or contribute in any way and her husband expected that the status quo would remain.

Kirsty was exhausted, resentful, and overwhelmed. She got into the habit of rewarding herself by having a large evening meal and a few glasses of wine every night. Then she would finally put her feet up and, at that point in time, she would have chocolates and biscuits and anything else she could get her hands on.

The label that she had given herself was "The Homemaker". What I did to help her was take that label away from her. I helped her to reframe her circumstances by showing her that she is just one of a number of adults in the house. There is no reason for her to be responsible for putting food on the table, washing everyone's clothes, or any of those tasks. She was busier than any of the other adults in the house and they needed to contribute.

Every member of Kirsty's family was capable of making a valuable contribution to the household. Initially, it was very difficult for her to surrender her role to the others – as they may not have done it as well – and to admit that she needed help, but that was what she had to do.

Kirsty subsequently had a conversation with every single person in the family and an agreement was made about what everyone would do and how they would contribute.

This meant that Kirsty could come home and not have to face the cooking and the chores. Once everyone began to contribute towards maintaining the household and it was no longer her "job", she did not feel overwhelmed or stressed. This meant that she did not feel that she had to resort to emotional eating and drinking alcohol unnecessarily.

She was able to make conscious choices about exactly what she was eating and drinking. Having everybody pulling their weight helped her feel more relaxed, calmer, more serene, and a lot happier within herself.

The homemaker label was eliminated. At times, she was the one who did the cooking or the one who organised things, but she was no longer the person expected to do everything.

This strategy has worked and put her in a better, calmer place where she feels in control. Kirsty is now able to manage her eating so that she is losing weight and feeling better about herself.

Take some time to notice the daily stressors you have in your own life and know that life does not have to be like this! Find a way to get rid of those stressors so you do not have to deal with them day in and day out.

Power Points – Chapter 2

1. Removing labels from your identity allows you to explore all possibilities for who and what you can be.

2. Thinking outside the box broadens your horizon and gives you more options.

3. Starting to see yourself as more than your job title automatically opens up other possibilities, which become compelling reasons why you need to make changes in your life.

4. Flexibility is key to change and change is inevitable. The more flexible your thinking is, the more you can adapt and succeed within an ever-changing world.

5. Being passionate about all the different aspects of life will facilitate bringing that energy and passion into your work life.

MD ACTION 2

Now that you have ditched the label that is holding you back, you need to create a picture with all the different parts that make up your unique personality.

Write a list (be as descriptive as possible) of all the different people you can be. Are you a loving father, a sexy spouse, a caring son, a loyal friend, an average golfer, a beginner runner, a romantic poet, an avid reader, a wine connoisseur?

Beyond Labels

My Unique Identity	
Characteristic	Why is it Unique?

The purpose of this task is to discover all the different parts of who you are and who you can be, not just the part of you that works, stresses, or becomes anxious.

One way of performing this task is to think about work colleagues, friends, family, and acquaintances, and asking what role you play in their life and identifying the activities you enjoy.

Once you complete this task, the answers to the following questions will unfold:

Who are you really? Who are you really beyond your labels? What is at the very core of who you are?

3

Subconscious Creations

"Whatever you determine to be true in the subconscious becomes true for you."

Richard Hatch

Now that you have taken responsibility for everything that has happened in your life and you have identified the labels that are holding you back, you need to start becoming aware of the way that you are currently doing things.

The way that you do things is really a subconscious strategy. You are not aware of what this strategy is at the conscious level, but I can guarantee that there is a certain way that you do everything.

Whether it is the way that you shop, prepare dinner, or play out certain habits, you always do it a certain way. It is very important that you find out how you do these various things and bring them into your conscious awareness. Once these habits are in your conscious mind you can change them.

If you are not aware how you play out your habits and your behaviours, then it will be difficult to make the changes you need to make.

"How the hell do I do that?" I hear you ask.

"I don't know how I do things, I just do them!"

Your subconscious patterns are not easily identifiable because they are played out at the subconscious, not the conscious level. So, whenever I ask a client, "How do you do the problem?" they look at me quizzically because they do not know "how" they do it. They just do it. In other words, what is the step-by-step subconscious process that takes you from the Trigger, to the Thought, to the Emotion and then to the Behaviour?

Then we work it out, step by step by step:

STEP 1   What was the trigger?

STEP 2   What was the thought?

STEP 3   What was the emotion?

STEP 4   What was the behaviour?

So there is actually a logical process for this strategy. You need to notice the sequence of events unfolding from the trigger, to the thought, to the emotion, to the action itself.

You may not know what your subconscious strategies are because you have never bothered to find out, but from now on you will need to be mindful of your thoughts, patterns, feelings, and actions. With this awareness, your subconscious strategies will be uncovered.

Subconscious Strategies

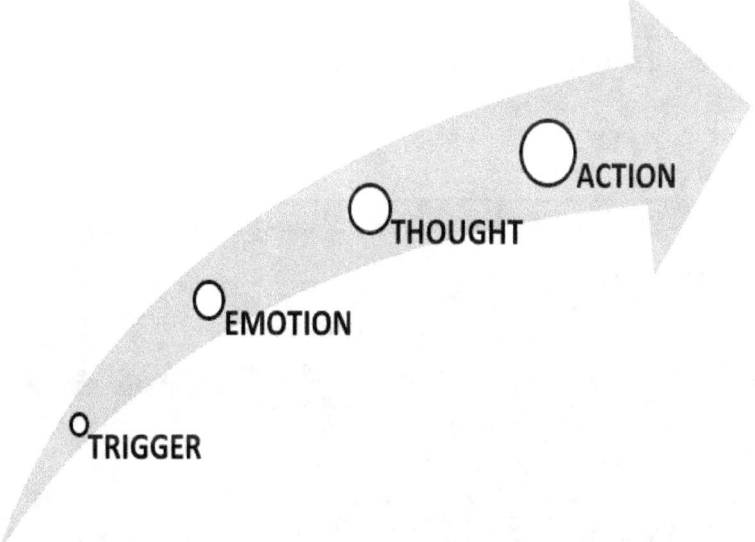

You need to be aware of the exact strategy and the sequence of events so that you can make some instant changes that will easily and effortlessly have a big impact.

You will need to get to the "low hanging fruit" first to achieve some quick wins.

Once you are aware of those subconscious strategies and you bring them up into your conscious awareness, you can then move forward and adopt more helpful strategies that will assist you in attaining your goals.

99 Bottles of Wine at the Mall – Liz

One of my clients Liz would buy a bottle of wine every day after work which she would drink that night.

Her strategy was that every day she went to the shops to get last-minute items for the evening's meal and would inevitably find herself buying a bottle of wine as well.

So her strategy would look something like this:

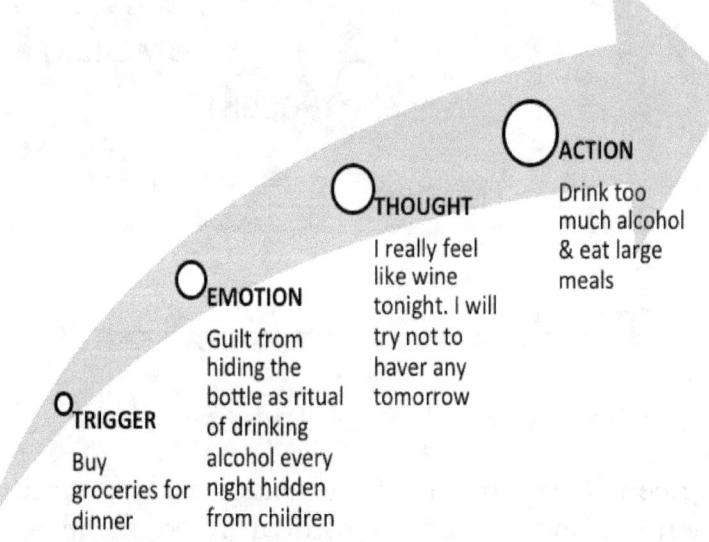

She tried to stop herself from buying a bottle of wine. Liz's strategy of going to the shops after work, buying groceries for dinner, and then also buying wine was so deeply entrenched in her subconscious mind that she found it very difficult not do it at a conscious level.

So I asked Liz to change one part of her strategy and *voila* – it became so easy for her.

Instead of buying her groceries for dinner after work, she bought them in the morning before work.

Her new strategy looked like this: before work —> go to shops —> buy groceries for dinner.

She had absolutely no desire for wine in the morning, so it was easy for her *not* to buy the alcohol. Liz went from drinking one bottle of wine per night to only 3 glasses every weekend! The best part about this new strategy was that it was easy and effortless. One small, strategic change achieved the desired result.

My Workmates are Driving Me Crazy – Joe

Joe is a Senior Data Analyst who is married, has five children (two of them diagnosed with Autism) and an elderly mother who lives in the family home.

When Joe first came to see me, he was highly stressed. His home life was frantic.

There was so much of Joe's life that was seemingly influenced by external factors, such as his senior government job. The last thing he wanted was to be controlled by an overbearing manager when he got to work. However, that's exactly what happened every single day. Every email he sent had to be approved by her first! This was his subconscious strategy.

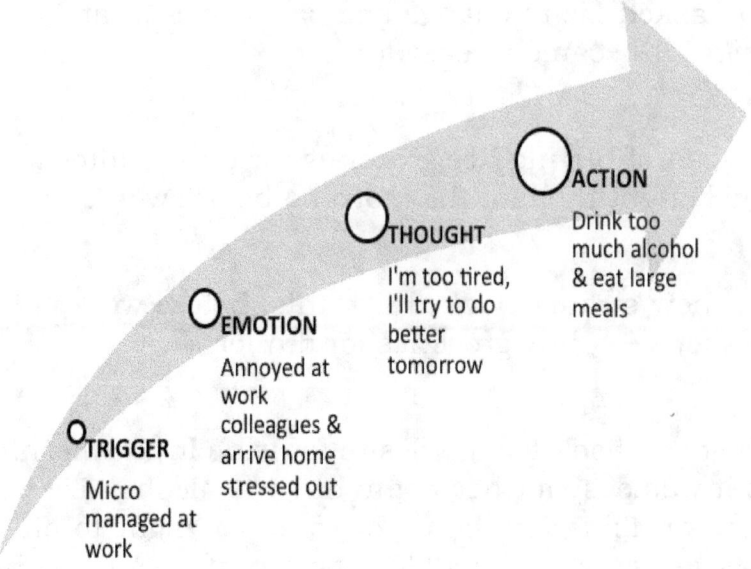

Together we worked at enabling Joe to set some clear boundaries in his workspace so that he arrived home in a completely different frame of mind.

Triggers

The trigger can be that you see something, heard something, or even smelt something, which triggers a thought, which triggers a feeling, which triggers an action.

That is a subconscious strategy.

It is important that you become aware of your triggers. Maybe you are exhausted and need to relax and you need to find some time in your day where you do not have any distractions. You just need to be still.

Perhaps you have had an unpleasant encounter at work and you need to reframe it and learn from it rather than pretending it did not happen by having a glass of wine. That does not solve the original problem; it will still be there for you to deal with the next day, along with the unwanted bonus of putting on the extra kilos around your waistline from the additional high caloric value of alcoholic drinks.

I am all about finding out what it is that needs to change at the very source of the issue. Not the symptoms, not the behaviours, but the source.

Emotions – What are they Trying to Tell You?
Your emotions are there to tell you something. They are there like flashing warning signals telling you that some changes need to be made.

Instead of noticing what your emotions are trying to tell you, you ignore them and try to make yourself feel better by eating food, drinking alcohol, smoking, or abusing drugs (prescription or illicit).

When you are aware of the emotions behind the actions, you can do something about satisfying the real need, not covering up the symptom.

Instead of using food and alcohol to cope with negative feelings, you notice what you are feeling and deal with that emotion. Food will never satisfy sadness, loneliness, boredom, depression, anger, or frustration.

Turning to food and alcohol may help you to feel better in the short-term and provide you with instant gratification, but it will never satisfy the underlying need. When you are feeling down, work out why and do something about it!

There is always something better to do than eat when you are not hungry. If you are feeling sad, watch a feel-good movie. If you are lonely, join a club – you will be surprised how many like-minded individuals you can connect with in your own area when you look for them. Have a look at meetup.com – this is a fantastic website with the purpose of helping groups of people with shared interests plan meetings and form offline clubs in local communities around the world.

If you are bored, start attending to those tasks that you never seem to have enough time to do. You have excess energy – use it!

Thoughts
The chatter in your head is another link in your subconscious strategy. By becoming aware of the chatter in your head and being mindful of the names and labels you give yourself such as "fat", or "lazy" or whatever, you can then stop those thoughts in their tracks, and switch them to kinder ones.

By discovering these subconscious patterns, you can develop strategies to break them and take purposeful actions in a mindful way.

Studies have shown that the subconscious mind controls more than 90% of our behaviours. This means that, if you do not make the effort to notice what is happening below the surface, you will be oblivious to what you are doing most of the time.

3 Subconscious Creations

You need to become mindful of your subconscious thoughts because your subconscious thinking dictates most of your behaviour. If you take the time to notice your thoughts and feelings and become consciously aware, then you can recognise where changes need to be made to these patterns.

The subconscious mind refers to that part of the mind that you are not aware of. Most of you have a good understanding of what you need to do to lose extra weight and get fit at the conscious level. It really is a basic equation of energy in and energy out. However, your habits, your beliefs, your emotions, and your values are all kept in the subconscious mind and influence the action that you are taking.

An example of how your subconscious mind works is when you first learn to drive a car; you are very aware of where your hands are placed, which mirror to look at, etc. After a while, you get from point A to point B without knowing how you got there. This is because it all happens at the subconscious level. It becomes automatic.

Another example is when you arrive home from work and you automatically reach for a glass of wine. You do not take any notice of what your thought processes are, what you are feeling, or what has been going on for you during the day; you are just in the habit of reaching for that wine at the end of the day.

If you consciously decide to stop drinking wine on a weeknight but you continue to repeat the same behaviour of having that glass of wine every night, you are ignoring what is happening under the surface.

The Welcome Home Wine Habit – Steve

One of my clients, Steve, who is a CEO of a mid-sized company, would in the past always start drinking wine the moment he arrived home.

When Steve started my "Take Control & Live Strong" program he agreed to implement a few AFDs (Alcohol-Free Days) in his week, and together we agreed on the days of the week that would be declared AFDs.

On one particular day that was supposed to be an AFD, he decided to ignore the agreement we made and went ahead and had a glass of wine. When I asked him "Why?", he said it was because the day at work had been particularly difficult. He felt stressed and thought that the only real option for him was to revert back to his old strategy of 'winding down' and having a glass of wine.

I then asked him to not have a glass of wine next time he arrived home feeling stressed from work. So, the next time he arrived home stressed, he knew that he could not have a glass of wine and then he had to work out why he was feeling stressed. He went through the events of the day and figured out how he could do something differently for the next day for a different outcome.

By changing the strategy, Steve was able to be effective in managing his emotions and the actions that he needed to take. He could become empowered and stay on track with the conscious changes he was making.

Takeaway Food Strategy

It could be that you have decided that you will not have any takeaway food at all this week – but, when the time comes, it is a different story. It is the end of the day, you have arrived home exhausted, your sugar levels are low, you are hungry, and you have not had a chance to have a proper lunch. You think to yourself, "I deserve whatever I want ...", and all your good intentions go out the window! Familiar scenario?

If you were mindful of your subconscious thoughts, perhaps you could have switched your thoughts to, "That is right, I do deserve better than that. My body deserves a healthy meal that will help me feel better. And when I get home, I am going to have a tuna salad which is quicker than going out to the pizza shop".

Can't Have a Coffee Without Cake Habit – Rod

Rod worked in a large company in the Melbourne CBD and at the ground floor level of his building there was a cafe. When Rod felt he needed a break, twice or three times daily, he would go to the cafe for a coffee. More often than not, he would grab something to eat with that coffee. It could be a muffin, Florentine biscuit or a piece of cake. All of these food items added up to excess calories and excess weight.

We determined that his subconscious strategy was that he chose to go down to have a coffee when he was feeling overwhelmed with work. The moment he was feeling that he had too much to do, he would postpone the task of deciding what he had to do next by giving himself a break and going downstairs, have a coffee and a sweet.

This bad habit was getting played out every time he felt overwhelmed. So, what we needed to do was actually break that strategy.

I told Rod that the next time he was feeling overwhelmed, he needed to get up and have a quick short walk down the road and back.

What this new strategy did was serve the purpose of clearing his mind and provided him with the clarity needed to focus on the task at hand. When he got back to his desk, he was ready to take focused action. This was a great strategy because, apart from the fact that Rod was no longer eating copious amounts of muffins, he got some regular exercise as well! This was a healthy strategy for both mind and body, and the incidental exercise was an added bonus!

Just to reiterate, that trip to the cafe did not seem like it was a strategy he was undertaking – it had become a habit for him to give himself that break. What he did not realise was that stress was triggering that need. What I did was to create an empowering alternative for him to alleviate the stress, so he did not need the cake and coffee to feel better. There was another way; just to go for a very short, brisk walk, no more than 5–10 minutes, which is the same amount of time he spent getting his coffee and muffin and going back to his desk.

Whatever you are doing and whatever triggers you have, you need to introduce an alternative and empowering way of dealing with that particular issue, which will help you rather than hold you back.

3 Subconscious Creations

What if I keep doing the same destructive behaviour even when I become aware of what I am thinking?

As you become aware of your subconscious strategies, you do need to make some decisions about making some changes. Some conscious effort is required, but it will be easier for you now that you have awareness and know what you are dealing with.

It takes practice and repetition for an action to become a habit. You will need to be conscious of your actions and keep repeating them until they become habits. Keep going with the new strategies until you make them stick.

When you are honest with what is really going on underneath the surface, you can do something about it.

"Whatever we plant in our subconscious mind and nourish with repetition and emotion will one day become a reality."
Earl Nightingale

Power Points – Chapter 3
1. You do things a certain way, acting on triggers, emotions and habits.

2. Your subconscious mind generates 90% of your actions and reactions.

3. You need to bring your subconscious thoughts and actions to your conscious mind in order to make changes to the way you act and react.

4. You must listen to what your emotions are telling you about how you feel and react to certain triggers in your life.

5. You must develop new strategies and new ways of responding to your triggers to make lasting changes in your life.

MD ACTION 3

To help you uncover your subconscious strategies, complete the table below and identify a list of behaviours that you would like to change.

Choose the behaviour you want to change first and bring up those subconscious strategies into your conscious mind.

Behaviour That I Would Like to Change					
Behaviour	Trigger	Thought	Emotion	Action

What are the triggers? What happens before or causes you to undertake the behaviour?

What are your thoughts before you undertake the behaviour?

What emotions are present?

What actions do you take?

4

False Perceptions

"The world is full of magic things, patiently waiting for our senses to grow sharper."

W.B. Yeats

Managing your emotions will help you manage your unhealthy habits. It is very likely that you are eating certain foods and drinks due to exhaustion, stress and anxiety.

Emotions are based on perceptions. Your perceptions are based on your unique filtering system.

You interpret the events in your life based on this unique filtering system.

The way this works is that, as human beings, our five senses are constantly taking in information in terms of what we see, hear, taste, touch and smell.

If it were possible to process all the information that comes our way, we would be processing an average of about 6 million bits of information per second. That is way more information than the conscious mind can possibly cope with, the information must pass through a number of filters first.

The filtering system within the subconscious mind deletes information that it is not interested in. It then sorts the remaining information into groups and distorts it according to your values, beliefs and habits, which are based on your past experiences and prior conditioning. Once the information is filtered in this way, it is reduced down to approximately 134 bits per second, which is then grouped into approximately 7 chunks of information.

Consequently, out of the 6 million bits of information per second that hit your senses, only 134 bits per second are actually absorbed by you and much of that is distorted through the process.

You can see that your perception can never be reality. These filters are what make every person and the way they perceive the world around them unique. No two people in the world filter information in the same way.

Why Do You Need to Know About Your Unique Filtering System?

Your perceptions are based on the way you filter the information around you. Perceptions lead to negative emotions, which lead to unwanted behaviours such as overeating and excessive drinking.

If you can learn to manage your perceptions, you will be able to better manage your emotions and therefore, learn to control unwanted behaviour.

Once you understand that your perceptions can never precisely reflect reality, due to missing, generalised, and distorted information, you will not be so committed to one rigid viewpoint. You will be able to give a different meaning to the events going on in your life. As your perspective changes by interpreting the event positively, this will help you move towards your goals rather than away from them.

Understanding that your perception is just your perception – nothing more, nothing less – will also help you see situations from other people's perspectives. Changing your perspective and seeing events from the other party's point of view will diffuse highly charged emotions and reduce stress. It will help you have positive relationships with your friends, family and colleagues. When you reconsider your perception, you can then see your situation from many different angles.

Once you accept and understand that different people have different values and other peoples' values don't have to be in line with yours, you can then respect their view of the world without agreeing with it. This attitude will give you a harmonious outlook on life and you will feel more positive.

What I am saying here is that you need to respect the other person's view of the world – not only understand it, but also really respect it. Allow yourself to see things from their perspective and allow them to have a completely different opinion from yours. When we respect other peoples' right to have their own opinion, we are not going to become so emotionally entangled in the need to be right.

> *"The more I see, the less I know for sure."*
> **John Lennon**

You are No Longer Required – Bob

Bob was a stressed-out CEO; he drank too much, and we made an agreement that there would be no drinking on certain days of the week. In other words, Monday through to Thursday would be classified as AFDs (Alcohol Free Days).

It was Wednesday and Bob had a particularly bad day, as he had had a large disagreement with a rather aggressive supplier, Steve. The story was that Steve was told his services were no longer required and he would not accept it.

Bob thought that Steve was being rude and obnoxious, as he would not accept his decision, and he didn't want to be rude back, so the discussions were longer than they needed to be and were quite taxing on Bob. Bob did not want to respond in an aggressive way because that wasn't in his nature. By the time Bob went home, he was feeling angry and stressed and resorted to drinking far too much alcohol.

Bob's story was that he had had a 'hard day' and 'needed a drink'. Bob needed to understand that his perception that Steve was rude and obnoxious was just his perception, not a fact.

An alternative, more empowering perspective, could have been that there was 'nothing personal' about it. Steve was just doing his job, as he wanted to retain the business and he was not going to give up without a fight for his livelihood. Bob's perception was that Steve was just being rude and that he was not going to stoop to his level and, therefore, the conversation went for much longer than it needed to.

What Bob needed to do was to distance himself from the situation and perhaps respond to the supplier in the same way and the same manner that he had been talked to. In other words, Bob would have been better off to say, "It's nothing personal, but this is the way it's going to be."

No justifications. No excuses.

Bob needed to stop the conversation and respond in the same manner he had been spoken to in the first place. If he had done that, he would not have taken it so personally. It was just a business discussion – nobody was being rude or obnoxious to him. The day did not have to be hard or difficult. The conversation would have been much quicker, easier to deal with, and less stressful than the way it played out.

Negative events happen to most of us and they will continue to happen, but it is the way that we react to these events that is important. The filtering system where information is generalised, deleted and distorted can actually be altered.

You can achieve the outcome you want in order to think, feel, and behave differently. The big lesson here is that, no matter whether the event is positive or negative, *YOU* are in control of the way you react to it.

How do you take control of your emotions?

You need to step outside yourself and observe the situation from a distance.

This is called dissociation. When you see the situation from outside yourself and you dissociate, then you do not associate with the emotion and you can see things from an objective point of view. When you are feeling the emotion, you allow the emotion to dictate your behaviour or response.

Taking control of your relationships and emotions will result in less need to use food and alcohol to numb out the emotions and will bring calmness and serenity into your life.

What if you do not know how to perceive the situation in another way apart from the way that you are currently filtering the situation?

4 False Perceptions

There is a positive way to perceive every situation. Even people who have suffered physical, mental, or emotional abuse can take something positive from the situation, even if it is about helping others who have been in the same situations as themselves.

What if seeing events from other people's perspective does not help the relationship because the other party is not prepared to change?

This is not about changing other people's behaviour or reactions to events. Taking control of your life and making sure that you run your life (and your life does not run you) is all about empowering yourself to feel a certain way – no matter what anybody else does. This is not about changing other people's behaviour; it is about changing the way you think and react so that the emotional turmoil is replaced with feelings of peace within you, allowing yourself to feel better about the situation.

What if you have fundamental problems with accepting a colleague's view of the world?

If you stubbornly refuse to accept and respect the other person's view of the world, this will be to your detriment, as no one else has your own unique filtering system. It would be to your benefit to understand, accept, and to respect other people's views of the world. When you truly understand your colleague's view, you will be able to influence them, as you can communicate in a manner that they can relate and positively respond to.

Once you understand and respect their view of the world, you can see things from their perspective and talk in a language that resonates with them. By doing that – by speaking their language – you have the ability to truly communicate with them.

Power Points – Chapter 4

1. Our brains filter a huge amount of information through various filters. This information can be distorted by our past experiences and values.

2. Perception is not reality. No two people will perceive information the exact same way.

3. We need to commit to trying to understand another person's viewpoint in order to be less rigid in our beliefs.

4. Learning to dissociate from negative situations allows us to view them impartially and even put a positive spin on the way we view the event.

5. We need to respect and understand others' viewpoints and speak their language in order to truly communicate with them.

MD ACTION 4

What I would like you to do now, before reading the next chapter, is identify three significant negative events in your life.

4 False Perceptions

What are your significant negative life events?

What meaning did you give to it at the time?

What positive meaning could you give to that event now?

Significant Negative Life Events		
Significant Negative Life Event	What Negative Meaning Did You Give That Event at the Time?	What Positive Meaning Can You Give it Now?

EXAMPLE

Event:	Tom – 47 year-old man, started at the gym to get fit; lasted for 3 weeks.
Old negative meaning:	"I'm too old."
New Positive meaning:	"I didn't have a big enough reason to see it through and now I do."

The same event and two completely different meanings.

One perspective limits Tom and stops him in his tracks, and the other helps him to regroup and try again.

5

Eureka Moments

"People think of these eureka moments and my feeling is that they tend to be little things, a little realisation and then a little realisation built on that."

Roger Penrose

So far ...

1. You have taken the responsibility to make some compelling changes in your life.

2. You have distanced yourself from all the labels that are holding you back from being the person that you can be.

3. You have understood that you have a unique filtering system with the way that you perceive the world around you.

4. You know that you can change that filtering system.

Now you are ready to discover the truth.

You are now ready for *eureka,* and when you discover the truth behind your bad habits, you can actually do something about them that will go to the source of the problem and eliminate it for good.

By discovering the source of the problem, you will be able to create strategies that result in permanent change as you work at overcoming the real cause of the problems in the area of your life you are not happy with. You will be able to go right to the root cause and fix it at the very core, rather than implementing a band-aid approach.

Band-aids simply do not work! They are temporary.

The makeshift temporary solutions only serve to frustrate you and reinforce the belief that you will not succeed because success seems to elude you every time you have tried to attain it. The reason success has eluded you is because the approach must be aligned with the 'actual' problem which has caused the symptoms.

For example, the symptoms might be anxiety and/or depression and emotional eating, but the underlying issue is a lack of self-worth.

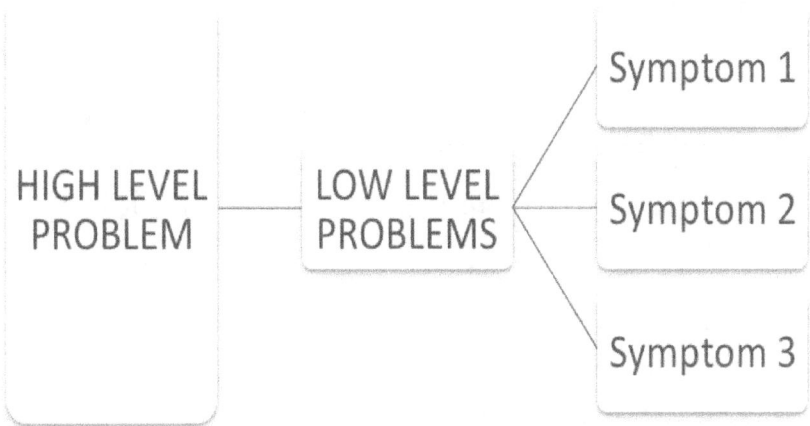

The Imbalance of Doing Business – Sarah

Sarah came to see me to lose weight.

Sarah had been to a doctor and had been diagnosed with Clinical Depression. The doctor told her that, since everything in her life was fine and there was no apparent cause for the way she felt, her depression was likely the result of a chemical imbalance.

Sarah believed that the depression was something she had to put up with, as it was out of her control. She simply needed me to help her lose weight. 20 minutes into the first session, it became apparent that everything was not as it seemed and there was an underlying sadness there. In fact, further questioning revealed that Sarah was very unhappy in her marriage. This was a secret she kept from everyone. She was ashamed to finally admit it.

Her unhappiness stemmed from years of emotional abuse from her husband. Overeating was the way she reacted to this abuse.

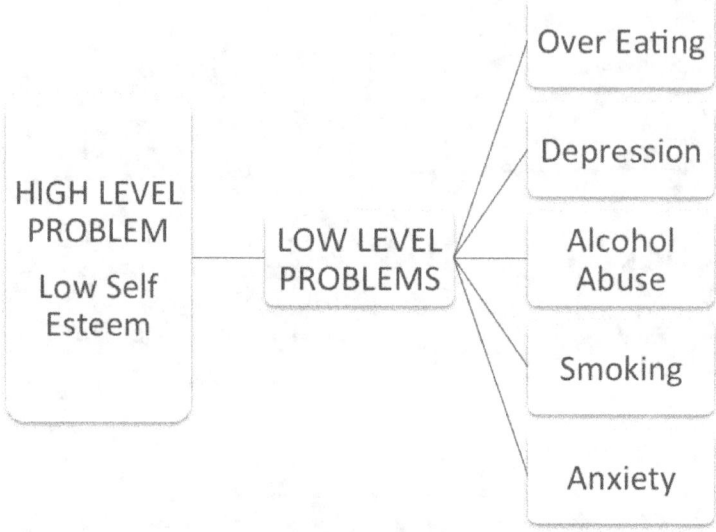

At that moment, Sarah had an *a-ha* moment as to why she was overeating. She dared not admit the truth to even herself – but once she did, she felt a burden lift from her shoulders.

When you have finally had your *a-ha* moment and discover the truth, you will release the frustration and the negative emotions that are blocking your ability to move forward.

Your *eureka* moment is that *a-ha* moment when the light bulb lights up and reveals the truth about what is holding you back from achieving your goals. Usually, they are your fears, habits and values that are all held at the subconscious level holding you back from moving forward.

You are going to feel like a weight has been removed from your shoulders, and this will allow your energy to flow towards the attainment of your goals.

Once Sarah finally admitted to herself that she was deeply unhappy, she had to step outside her comfort zone and do something about it. She designed some deal-breakers, whereby verbal abuse from her husband would no longer be tolerated.

If Sarah's husband continued to treat her in this manner, she would have to initiate separation proceedings, even though she had so many fears relating to the unknown on the other side. What Sarah now knew for sure was that things could not stay as they currently were.

Once all those fears and anxieties were worked through, there was no need to resort to emotional eating and smoking to feel better.

"There are only two mistakes one can make along the road to truth; not going all the way, and not starting."

Buddha

Eureka – I am Afraid of the Gym!

I returned from an overseas trip in October 2014 and I kept making excuses about returning to the gym. I thought I was too tired, or too busy to get straight back into it. So I sat myself down and asked myself a series of questions as if I was asking them to a client.

I asked myself:

Question:	"Why aren't I going to the gym?"
Answer:	"Because I am too busy catching up with everything, as I have left my business for 7 weeks."
Question:	"Is that really true – am I really catching up with work at 6.00am in the morning?"
Answer:	"No."
Question:	"Then why aren't I getting up to go to the gym like I used to before the holiday?"
Answer:	"Because my body is not accustomed to the intense exercise."
Question:	"What does that really mean?"
Answer:	"I won't be as good as I used to be. I won't be able to lift the weights I used to lift."

BINGO! There was my answer. I was afraid! I was afraid of confronting my physical limitations. Now that I knew the real reason I was not going, it sounded ridiculously silly.

That was an *a-ha* moment for me!

5   Eureka Moments

I did not want to face it. I did not want to go back to the gym, as I was concerned that I would only be able to lift half the weight that I used to prior to going on holidays. Once I realised that fear was the real reason – and not because I was tired or overwhelmed at being back to work – I knew that the solution was simple. I simply needed to overcome the fear.

I overcame my fear by acknowledging it and then taking action. The first session back was the hardest, the second was also hard, but by the third one I knew that I would be fine and began to feel comfortable within the session. If I did not get to the source of that issue, I would still be kidding myself about it today.

The Private Life of Global Publicity – Peter

Peter held a high profile job as a Global Publicity Manager for which he was handsomely paid. Peter seemed to have everything: a loving wife, gorgeous children, a beautiful home, and a high-paid and rewarding career. He was respected within his industry. He had a network of family and friends who loved him. Despite all these wonderful elements of his life, he suffered from depression.

What we uncovered in our sessions together was that Peter was subconsciously sabotaging his life because he did not believe he should have the perfect life. His parents had died at a young age so were not able to enjoy their lives. This was the root of his depression – guilt over losing his parents. Upon eliminating the guilt in our sessions, he finally became free of his depression.

When Peter first came to me, he thought he was not capable of culling his addictive behaviour. But once he realised that he was going about sabotaging himself simply because he was holding onto guilt, then he could do something about it. He could accept that this guilt was no longer necessary in his life and he was entitled to live life to the fullest and be happy.

As my expertise is weight loss and depression, the clientele that I attract usually have weight loss and depression problems. What is interesting is that people believe they are depressed because they are overweight and that when they lose weight, they will no longer feel depressed, when in fact the reverse is true. People generally engage in emotional eating when they are depressed.

The cause of the depression, anxiety, or stress must be dealt with first. In order to deal with those symptoms of emotional eating, you need to get to the source of the issue and eliminate it.

This is exactly the reason why diets do not work. Dieting only deals with the symptoms of overeating or drinking in excess. This tells you nothing about what caused those symptoms to appear in the first place.

So what if there is no *a-ha* moment?

What if there is not any great realisation?

Your *eureka* moment will come to you when you are ready to open yourself up to the possibility that maybe this is all about you. Everything that is going on in your life is about you. It is not about all the drama you are caught up with or that you have created. It is not about other people. Not your bosses, or your work colleagues. It is not about your spouse or your children. It is all about you.

The changes that you need to make within your life are well within your control.

What if when you make that *a-ha* moment ... the truth really hurts? Your subconscious mind has been trying to protect you from feeling hurt by providing you with false perceptions. But now, you are ready for change and ready to hear the truth. While the truth may hurt, it has to be dealt with so that you can move forward.

You might be thinking, "Well, what if I'm not prepared to go forward? What if I'm simply not ready?" My answer to that is that at least you know that you can make changes – you have a choice and you are not stuck.

A Life without Power – Mallory
Mallory came to see me for chronic depression. During the course of our sessions together, she had her *a-ha* moment. Mallory realised that she could feel good again.

It was the first time she had felt good about herself and her life.

Subsequently, she re-entered her family life, which meant that she had to begin to pull her weight around the house. She had to get out of bed, do some tasks, and organise some housework in her household of men – four sons and a husband.

While she suffered from chronic depression, Mallory had a reason, an excuse, and a story as to why she couldn't do all those things. She sat on the couch or stayed in bed while everyone around her did what needed to be done. Once she worked with me and I helped her become empowered, she realised that she didn't want to live like that.

She had not wanted all the responsibilities and all the work, so her subconscious mind responded by giving her depression. This meant that she had a very good reason as to why she didn't have to face up to her enormous responsibilities. She had a lot of secondary gain from having depression. She didn't know that at the time.

This wasn't a conscious decision. She didn't consciously decide to stay in bed. She didn't consciously decide to stay on the couch for the entire day watching television. Once she worked through the program with me, she realised that she did have the choice to change, but she was not yet ready for the change.

She realised that she could manage her depression if she wanted to and that she was no longer a victim of a disease that she had no power over. The truth is, we get in our own way. We have all the resources within us to move forward and make the changes we need to make. When we discover this truth and take it to heart, we become truly empowered.

Power Points – Chapter 5
1. Once you have your *eureka* moment, you realise the power lies within you to change things in your life.

2. Getting to the source of negative behavior allows you to have permanent solutions to your problems, rather than a temporary fix.

3. We give ourselves excuses or reasons why we are not living up to our potential when the real reasons stem from fear or other negative emotions.

4. Eliminating fear and guilt frees us to live to our potential.

5. You don't need to be a victim in your own story. You have the resources within you to change your story and make it a positive outcome.

MD ACTION 5

What I'd like you to do is to really consider what's holding you back.

What's holding you back from where you need to go?

Is it really your age?

Is it really your relationships?

Is it really your work circumstances?

Is it really your boss?

Or is there something else? Are you fearful of something? Are you fearful of going outside your comfort zone? Are you fearful of trying something new? What's really holding you back?

Do this exercise right now.

List everything that's holding you back from achieving your compelling outcome.

What are the negative consequences for holding on to these beliefs?

What must you do but don't want to do?

What's Holding You Back?		
List Everything That's Holding You back From Achieving Your Compelling Outcome	What Are the Negative Consequences for Holding on to These Beliefs?	What Must You Do But Do Not Want to Do?

6

It's Just BS

"Above all, be true to yourself, and if you cannot put your heart in it, take yourself out of it."
Hardy D. Jackson

Let's look at how far you've come!

- You have decided to make some major changes in your life.

- You have decided it is your responsibility to make those changes.

- You have decided that you will no longer accept labels that hold you back from moving forward and going outside your comfort zone.

- You have uncovered those subconscious creations, those strategies that you subconsciously do, without even realizing that you are doing them. You can become conscious of what your emotions are trying to tell you.

- You have understood that your perceptions can never be reality – they are just your perceptions and are nothing more than that.

- You have discovered the truth.

- You found the *eureka* moment – the absolute truth about what it is that is holding you back from moving forward.

Now that you've discovered the truth, you can see the reasons for not achieving your goals are BS! Yes, that's right! Those reasons are simply not true!

This realisation will help you overcome the self-imposed barriers that are getting in your way.

Every time you say a sentence and you say the word 'BUT' – that word stops you in your tracks and prevents you from doing what you need to do. Why? You have given yourself an excuse. When you see the *reasons* why you can't achieve your goals for the *excuses* that they really are, you will be truly liberated. You will be free to take action and start achieving your goals.

You will also become attuned to excuses that you make in other areas of your life and will stop making them as well. When you discover that the reasons you have been hanging onto for so long are not, in fact, true, you will then be in a position to address the real reasons for your procrastination.

The real reason that we remain stuck is usually about fear.

Perhaps the fear that you are not indispensable at work and your work place can actually function without you?

Perhaps the fear of admitting to yourself that there is an area of your life that you are not good at?

The Fear of Failure?
How wonderful would it be to be truly honest with yourself and learn your true limitations so that you can acknowledge your weaknesses and then have the opportunity to grow?

Obese employees experience higher levels of absenteeism due to illness than those employees who are within a normal weight range. And of course there are always perceived "reasons" as to why they become obese and stay obese. These employees need to understand that these reasons are just BS. They are just excuses.

If you don't admit to yourself that it is BS, there will always be a reason as to why you can't achieve your goals. But there never will be any results, so what is it that you want? Do you want to hang onto the reasons for not taking action? These reasons may be very good but nothing ever changes when you hold onto excuses. What do you really want? Remember, it's entirely up to you.

Reasons or Results?

You will always be able to find a reason as to why you can't take action and achieve your goals.

Many people believe they are too busy to exercise consistently or to make healthy food choices. And this BS stops you from moving forward and doing what's right for you, because you believe it.

Whenever anyone tells me they are too busy to exercise, I ask them whether they believe they are busier than former President Obama? When he was President of the United States, Obama faced a very busy schedule. He started every day by exercising anything from 45–90 minutes every day. Obama's former campaign manager told Web MD that his logic was, "The rest of my time will be more productive if you give me my workout time."

"I was once afraid of people saying, 'Who does she think she is?' Now I have the courage to stand and say, 'This is who I am.'"

Oprah Winfrey

Time does not discriminate. Time is distributed equally. There is not one person on this earth that has more time than anyone else. The truth is that we spend our time doing those things which matter to us most. We always manage to make time for whatever we consider to be important. Many of my clients don't allocate any time to their health at all when they first come to see me because they have placed greater value on being successful at work.

It's not that they don't have the time; it's that the time is allocated to other activities that are deemed to be more important or valuable.

The former Prime Minister of Australia, Tony Abbott, is another example of maintaining an intense fitness regime while maintaining a high-profile, busy job. In fact, Prime Minister Abbott kept his intense exercise regime even during the campaign for the National Election, which is run at a frenetic pace. The way he managed his time was to cycle from town to town so he could maintain his fitness, right through the election campaign.

There was no excuse. No BS. Can you get any busier than running for the highest office in the country? Yet he still found the time every single day to do what he needed to do.

It could be that you think that your occupation is unique, that nobody else understands your specific circumstances and that there is nobody else that could do the job that you do. Again, that's BS! Every single person's skills, knowledge and know-how can be replicated. Other people can be trained to do your work. The most effective people delegate appropriately so that everything runs smoothly without them. If you're not doing that, then you're not doing your job effectively.

When I was working as a manager, I saw my job as making myself redundant so that anyone could step into my role and produce the same results.

You may be asking, "What if you don't have the motivation to maintain an effective exercise regime?" Motivation is created when you have a big enough "WHY", a compelling reason as to why you want change in your life. When you can feel that you WANT, rather than HAVE to achieve your goals in your life, then you will be motivated towards taking action.

People will always take action when they have a strong emotion connected to their "why". There needs to be a reason as to why you need to do what you need to do. So, find your why. It could be that your why is that you want to be around for your children or your grandchildren and stand by their side during their life journey. I don't know your 'why', but you do!

What if you travel so much that it's impossible for you to establish a routine where good habits are maintained? Once again, if you make your health 'non-negotiable', then you will absolutely find a way.

I often travelled in my various roles when working in the corporate sector for 22 years. Since becoming fit, I would always find out the locations of changing rooms, showers, and places to work out before I arrived at the new location so that I could resume exercise immediately with no time lag in between working for different clients at different sites. This was my absolute number one priority before I began work at a new location. That way, I could get there early in the morning, go to the gym, go for a run, do whatever

I needed to do, then get back, have a shower, and be ready to start work on time.

I organised the logistics around where I was exercising and how I could get ready for my workday. No excuses. It didn't matter where I was going or whom I was working for. I wouldn't find the showers 'later on' or 'once I settled'; I would seek them out and discover where they were before I even began on **day one**.

It could be that your BS is all about thinking that you must entertain clients or family regularly forcing you to eat certain foods or drink certain alcohol. This is straight up BS! There is no implied requirement that states you must consume alcohol or eat more food than you need to for the sake of keeping clients, family or work colleagues happy!

What's the real reason beneath the BS here? Do you find that you relax more and are more sociable when you drink? What is it? Are you unable to manage your feelings of being overwhelmed or stressed any other way?

Honestly, what you are putting in your mouth has no impact on anyone, nor does it impact their experience.

You can be just as affable without consuming extra food or alcohol calories. There is no expectation for you to eat food or consume drinks that are unhealthy for you.

You might be asking, "What if nothing else interests me apart from my work?" Even if nothing else apart from your work interests you at this point in time, you need to be open-minded to the possibility that perhaps something else can interest you. If you just open the door wide enough for opportunities to be seen you might be surprised at how many interesting opportunities exist.

So get rid of the BS, strip it away. Every single time you hear the word "but" in your mind, ask yourself,

"Is that really true?"

"Is it really true that I am too old to lift weights?"

"Is it really true that I'm too busy to take 40 minutes out of my day?"

Did you know that if you only allocate one hour of your day, every single day, to exercise, that's just 4% of your day? Are you busier than former President Obama? Is it impossible for you to allocate 4% of your day towards your health?

I want you to ask yourself, "Is this really true?" And if it were really true, how awful would it be to be stuck and not have any options or anywhere to go?

If it's not really true, then let's get real and find out what you need to do to move forward in life.

The Priority of Health – Colin
Colin was a senior executive at one of the biggest banks in the country. When Colin first came to see me

his health had deteriorated to the extent where he had already had a heart attack as well as prostate cancer.

Colin decided that his Number 1 priority would be to get his health back on track. The number one objection he would raise with regards to exercising consistently and daily was his time. He believed that as he was responsible for the bank's biggest multimillion dollar global projects, he needed to be available to all the project managers that reported to him from the early morning until quite late at night and that there was no time for him to exercise.

Colin loves swimming so the solution we created was a scheduled daily time slot in his calendar where he effectively made an appointment with himself to swim. The key was that the scheduled time slot was not during the mid-day rush when everybody else was also hitting the gym. The scheduled time slots were made during times when everybody else was at work. This way, he could get to the gym and back with minimum fuss and time. He wasn't waiting in queues. He went and did what he had to do and got back.

I impressed upon him that these scheduled appointment times for his daily swim were more important than any other scheduled meetings in his calendar. The scheduled swim times were usually at 10:30am in the morning or in the late afternoon and he was back within the hour.

In actual fact, Colin became more productive than ever before because the project managers that reported to him, who were often asking him questions and demanding his time, were gone during that lunch hour. He now had that time to catch up with his work and be productive during the time when most people were not there. His daily swim also reinvigorated him and allowed him to view issues with renewed clarity and focus. His daily swim cleared his head and he felt better physically and mentally than ever before.

There's always a reason as to why you can't do something. It's just an excuse, it's just BS, you need to get rid of it.

Power Points – Chapter 6

1. The reasons you make up for not achieving your goals are not true, they are BS!

2. We hold ourselves back by coming up with reasons, which are really excuses.

3. We can let go of excuses and make our good health a priority.

4. The real truth is that we are not too busy to allocate 4% of our day to our good health.

5. We are all given an equal measure of time and you will use your time for what you deem to be most important.

6. Making your health a priority in your day will benefit you in all aspects of your work and life.

MD ACTION 6

The exercise that I'm asking you to do now is to get real about time. I want you to separate your activities into these categories. Have a look at the table below.

Distractions

List all your distractions. What are they? Facebook, YouTube, Movies, TV programs? How many hours in a day do you spend on those distractions and what is the percentage of these hours in your day?

Get Real About Time		
List Your Distractions	Hour / Day	%
TOTAL		
Urgent – Not Important	Hour / Day	%
TOTAL		
Urgent & Important	Hour / Day	%
TOTAL		
Not Urgent – Very Important	Hour / Day	%
TOTAL		

Urgent ... but not Important

Next let's look at that category where you do urgent tasks that are not important.

They might be urgent because you have left them to the last minute, but they are not actually important. Tasks like filing paperwork, household tasks or shopping.

They become urgent because if you don't do them, you can't find what you need when you need it, your home becomes cluttered and messy or you run out of basic supplies. They are not important. They have only become important because you have left them unattended for so long.

Urgent ... and Important!

Urgent and important tasks have also been left to the last minute. They are important tasks like preparing your income tax. List the hours that you spend on these tasks and what percentage of your time you spend per day.

Not Urgent and ... Very Important!

There are tasks that are very important but not urgent. It is vital that you do these tasks BEFORE they become urgent. These are the tasks that make the most difference to your productivity.

That's where most of your time should be spent, on important, but not urgent tasks.

Get Real About Time

- Your distractions are obvious time wasters.

- Urgent, but not important tasks have become unnecessary time wasters.

- When completing your urgent and important tasks there may be an enormous amount of stress because you have to do very important tasks in a very short period of time.

In the final category of not urgent and very important tasks is ideally where you should be spending most of your time so that you can manage your time rather than reacting to an emergency due to an imminent deadline. Doing the most important task for that day first thing will save you time later on, because the task has not yet become urgent. You have addressed it and you've dealt with it before it becomes urgent.

Most of you are probably thinking that I have no idea of what your schedule is and that there is no way you can fit in a consistent and regular exercise schedule. I'm here to tell you that that is absolute BS!

For me to attain my desired fitness levels, I need to be up at 5:06 every single morning. There is no other way for me to meet my fitness goals.

I have two alarms. One alarm is beside my bed and one is located where I need to physically get out of bed to turn it off. When the alarms ring, I get up. I have my runners, top and shorts ready. There is no thinking required. It's a no brainer.

It becomes a simple matter of putting those clothes on, getting out of the door, and just doing it, no matter what the weather is or how I feel about it. This is my commitment to my health, and I am sticking with it.

My alarm clocks are set for 5:06 am and 5:09 am every morning, no matter what time I have gone to sleep on the previous evening. I simply must be up at 5:06 am in the morning to do the exercise I need to do. You too can arrange a time where it's a non-negotiable activity. It's always best for you to plan your exercise around the morning, because then it's out of the way, it's done and you know that you are set up mentally for the rest of the day.

Otherwise, if you plan to exercise at lunchtime or after work, family matters, urgent meetings or a crisis, which needs your attention could get in the way. However, if you have done your exercise in the morning there is nothing that can hold you back, from you getting out of bed, putting your runners and training gear on and just moving. You need to have your training gear ready, your runners ready, so that you are ready to go. There is no holding back. The moment your alarm goes off, you get up, get out of bed, and you GO!

7

Balancing Act

"If you're interested in balancing work and pleasure, stop trying to balance them. Instead make your work more pleasurable."

Donald Trump

Now that you know all the excuses, stories and reasons you've been telling yourself are simply BS, you can work out how to have a balancing act.

Your mental and physical energy needs to be aligned so that you can have the harmonious balance that you need so much in your life.

So many people invest time and energy in matters that are not important to them and don't make them happy. This leads to resentment and feeling overwhelmed.

Resentment arises when you spend most of your time doing what you feel you have to do rather than what you want to do.

There is no doubt that we all must do things that we do not want to do when we are pursuing our goals.

For instance, even though you may not want to exercise, you must do it so that you can attain your goals.

What I am referring to is all those other activities that do not support your higher vision. Do you find that you are saying "Yes" to events when you really want to say "No", then end up doing activities according to someone else's agenda? Before you know it, you are resentful and annoyed.

Ask yourself these questions:

"Is what I am being asked to do important to me?"

"Is this activity going to take me towards one of my goals or not?"

If the answer to both of those questions is "No", maybe you need to learn to very politely say "No"!

If you don't spend your time doing what makes you happy and instead spend your time on what other people expect you to do, you're very likely to regret it.

> *"There's no such thing as work-life balance. There are work-life choices, and you make them, and they have consequences."*
>
> **Jack Welch**

It is your job to make sure that you feel fulfilled and happy with what you *choose* to do rather than what others are telling you that you *should* do. Your values need to be front of your mind so that you place your energy into actions that take you closer to your life's purpose.

Work-life balance is used to describe the balance between an individual's work and personal life. Studies show that the participation rate in sport and physical recreation was as high as for those whose work commitments allowed them to also meet other family and community responsibilities.

What this shows is that, where people have found a way around their work commitments so that they have more time to spend on themselves, they are more likely to do physical activity.

Regret-Proof Yourself!
Regret # 1: Not Living a True Life!
The biggest regret people report having at the end of their life is the regret of not having the courage to live a life true to themselves and instead living a life that others expected of them.

Regret # 2: Not Enough Family Time!
People regret that they work too much and regret not spending more time with their partner or children.

Regret # 3: Not Enough Travel!
Studies show that many elderly people regret not traveling earlier on in their life at a time when they could actually enjoy the places they saw and the experiences they had. They kept putting things off, making excuses as to the reasons why they couldn't travel earlier. They waited till they retired and their bones ached and they had a number of annoying and inconvenient ailments.

What regrets will you have on your deathbed if nothing changes?

When I asked myself this question, the answer came to me immediately.

"Paris!"

I would regret not going to Paris.

7   Balancing Act

I decided I was going that year!

Work-life balance is a concept which includes proper prioritisation between career, ambition and lifestyle (health, pleasure, leisure, family, spiritual development). Personally, I think that the paradigm has shifted for work-life balance.

As time goes on, people are increasingly getting rewarded for work in areas they enjoy as opposed to having a job that simply serves the purpose of paying the bills. Mobile technology allows us to conduct work in many places and at home. The distinction between work time and pleasure time isn't easily identifiable these days.

The distinction between work and pleasure has become quite blurred. For example, Lisa, a business coach, tends to invite her clients to personal parties that she has because she loves her work so much that these clients have become her friends.

In my view, the importance is not in ensuring that every area of your life is balanced, but rather that you are spending most of your time in the areas of your life that are most important to you.

This is the key factor.

In order to determine how to allocate your time to those tasks that you value most and are the most important to you, you need to ask the following question:

What is important in my life?

Find at least 6 areas that are important to you.

And then prioritise each and every area according to its importance at this time in your life.

You must be completely honest with yourself so that you can work with your values, not with the values of other people or society in general.

For example, it could be that you don't spend much time with your family – and that may be OK for you. However, if being with family is your number one value and you aren't allocating enough time with family, then this is going to lead to a gap in your level of life satisfaction.

7 Balancing Act

It's Just a Matter of Priorities – Lisa

As a successful business coach, Lisa recently told me that at this time in her life she valued her business more than her family. She placed the success of her business above her husband, her small children, and her mother. And this made it very easy to allocate her time to her business first without guilt. It's not to say that she didn't love her family; it's just that, at this point in time, she placed greater value on her business than on her family.

Her husband's prime responsibility was to look after the children and hers was to establish a successful business, which is what she achieved. What impressed me most with this business coach is that her actions were completely aligned to her values. She used her time according to her most important values without guilt and regret.

At times, life gets in the way of spending time on the areas of life that we value the most. For example, one of my clients, Nicola, felt unhappy that she wasn't seeing her friends regularly, as she spent most of her time at work or the theatre group where she was a cast member for a number of productions.

I suggested she take a proactive approach and organise catch-ups with her friends rather than waiting for them to invite her. Rather than waiting to be invited to a catch-up that someone else has organised, she started organising the social activities with her friends. Once she got into the routine of regularly catching up with friends, she then enjoyed the time she spent on other activities, such as work, as there was no longer an unfulfilled need.

What's interesting is that many of my clients say that health is their number one value, but when it comes down to it, this is not the case at all. Exercise time or pre-planned meals is the first to be sacrificed when life gets hectic. What this tells me is that, even though my clients say or think they value health above all else, they are spending no consistent quality time on this part of their life. It's not until they get sick that they actually decide to do something about their health.

When I started my fitness regime and began to exercise consistently, it became such an automatic habit that my family expected me to dedicate time to exercise every day. They just knew that this was something that I was never going to give up. No matter what it was that they needed from me, my absolute priority was exercise.

I always make sure that my exercise time doesn't negatively affect important family time. If I go for a walk with a friend, it is always after 8pm when the family is doing their own thing. It would never be during precious dinner time.

Exercise is very important to me, but making sure that I'm sitting down for dinner at the dinner table with my family is even more important. So I make sure that those things I value so much work alongside each other. I would never go for a walk or run during dinnertime, because that's family time. But I will make sure I get up that extra hour earlier in the morning and do whatever I need to do before it affects the rest of my family.

Power Points – Chapter 7

1. We're striving to achieve balance between our work and personal life.

2. We often allow ourselves to expend energy on things that don't align with our goals.

3. Learning to say "No" is an important skill to stay on course with our purpose.

4. Allocating time to exercise means making it a non-negotiable appointment each day. No excuses. We just do it.

5. Giving our energy to our priorities means that we are not deterred by other situations that arise. We don't allow ourselves to get off track from our goals.

MD ACTION 7

The Life Satisfaction Assessment measures the time you spend on each key life interest per week together with how satisfied you are in each of the areas. Please complete the chart (on the next page) by identifying how much time you spend on average each week. Then place a number in the box that best represents the level of satisfaction you have with each area (with 1 being the least and 10 being the most).

Your home play for this chapter will reveal exactly where you need to make improvements in your life.

STEP 1 Complete the Life Satisfaction Assessment below to identify the areas in your life where you have a low level of satisfaction.

STEP 2 If you have a low level of satisfaction in a specific area, this means it's a value that requires your attention.

STEP 3 Determine how you can improve the level of satisfaction in these areas.

Perhaps you need to increase the time spent on these areas or improve the quality of the time that is spent. For example, rather than increasing time spent at home, it may be sufficient to organise weekends away with the whole family or to organise date nights out with your partner.

Life Satisfaction Assessment		
Life Interest	Time Spent Each Week	Level of Satisfaction 1 to 10
Physical		
Mental		
Emotional		
Spiritual		
Business / Career		
Finance		
Health		
Family / Frienships		
Intimate Relationships		
Personal Growth		
Fun / Recreation		

8

Target Practice

"It is for us to pray not for tasks equal to our powers, but for powers equal to our tasks, to go forward with a great desire forever beating at the door of our hearts as we travel toward our distant goal."

Helen Keller

We have discussed the importance of living your life according to what is important to you and aligning those values with how you spend your time.

Now it's time to get very clear about what your target is, because you cannot hit the target unless you know what the target looks, sounds and feels like.

Many people know what they DO NOT want, but not many people know what it is that they actually DO want. When people come to see me, they are very clear about what they do not want because they have connected it with the emotional pain of their situation.

"I don't want to be embarrassed with the way I look"

"I am sick and tired of feeling exhausted"

"I don't want to be angry anymore"

However, it is not clear to these people what it is that they DO want. People generally focus on what they do not want, and as long as they do that, that's exactly what they get. Self-talk about not wanting stress, anxiety, depression, a busy life, being overweight, being unhappy, etc., means that their thoughts and feelings are immersed in what they do not want. This usually results in getting exactly that which they are trying to avoid.

Focusing on what you do not want will very likely get it for you. You tend to get what you focus on; for example, if you focus on not getting stressed, you're still focusing on the concept of 'stress'. What you need to focus on is clarity and serenity and not on "not being stressed", as the subconscious mind does not process negatives such as "not" before a word. It focuses on the word itself.

EXAMPLE

"I will not allow myself to get stressed"

Your subconscious mind will only hear '**stress, stress, stress!**'

The subconscious mind also learns and retains memories best with symbols and pictures. Therefore, if you give your subconscious mind a specific picture of your compelling outcome, your subconscious mind will believe it to be true. It starts to behave like you are already the person you are visualising.

If the subconscious believes that you are a fit, healthy, and strong person, then it's not going to engage in behaviours that contradict that persona such as driving through a fast food outlet on the way home.

When you have visualised what you want in detail, opportunities that you may not have previously noticed are now within your radar.

Employees are motivated by clear goals and appropriate feedback, and studies show that working towards a goal provides a major source of motivation to reach that goal, which in turn improves performance.

When people tell me about lacking motivation, quite often the reason is that their "why" (the reason for attaining the goal) is not big or clear enough. My clients know that they need to lose weight before they come to see me. But they haven't been able to shift their behavioural patterns to achieve their goals because there wasn't a big enough reason for them to make the changes they needed to make.

Once I established an emotional association to their reasons, they were then motivated to take the action they needed in the direction of those goals.

A Crystal Clear Reason – Crystal

Crystal is a senior staff member at an exclusive all-girls school. Even though she knew her weight was climbing to dangerous levels, she justified her lack of discipline over her food intake and physical activity by believing that she was far too busy to do anything about it.

Everything changed when Crystal became a grandmother and she started to feel physically restricted in her ability to look after her grandchild.

She became increasingly concerned about not being around for her grandson as he got older and was plagued by the thought that, if she continued to carry this amount of excess weight, she may not be around to see her grandchildren get married. Her parents had attended all the weddings of their own grandchildren, and she wanted to be able to do the same.

Crystal asked me whether I thought she was going to be around for her own grandchild's wedding and the answer I gave her was, "That depends on the choices you make today!"

Crystal suddenly had a very big "why" as to the reason she had to lose the weight. She had to lose the weight to be around for her grandchildren, because she wanted this more than anything in the world.

She wanted this more than that extra bit of cake; she wanted this more than that extra glass of wine. Crystal proceeded to lose over 35 kilos over the next few months.

There was an extensive study conducted at the Seoul 1988 Olympic Games on mind training. In this study, 1,200 track and field athletes were surveyed to determine what the difference was between those athletes that had qualified for the Olympic Games and those that hadn't qualified.

The habits and skills of the 1,200 athletes were analysed and it was found that across the sample group all the athletes were very similar. The analysis of the data found that there was only one differentiating factor between those that qualified for the Olympics Games and those that didn't.

The athletes that did qualify spent a considerable amount of time undertaking mental training.

What this shows us is that, when we have a very clear goal in mind and visualise that goal, it's very likely that we will attain it. We've brought it into our conscious awareness and we take definitive actions that lead us there.

The Matthews Study 2003 – Dr Gail Matthews Ph. D. (Psychology Professor Dominican University of California)

Research recently conducted by Matthews shows that people who wrote down their goals, shared this information with a friend, and sent weekly updates to that friend, were on average 33% more successful in accomplishing their stated goals than those who merely formulated goals.

Group 1 was asked to simply think about the business-related goals they hoped to accomplish within a four-week block and to rate each goal according to: difficulty, importance, the extent to which they had the skills and resources to accomplish the goal, their commitment and motivation, and whether they had pursued the goal before (and, if so, their prior success).

Groups 2–5 were asked to write their goals and then rate them on the same dimensions as given to Group 1.

Group 3 was also asked to write action commitments for each goal.

Group 4 had to both write goals and action commitments and also share these commitments with a friend.

Group 5 went the furthest by doing all of the above plus sending a weekly progress report to a friend. Broadly categorised, participants' goals included: completing a project, increasing income, increasing productivity, improving organisation, enhancing performance/

achievement, enhancing life balance, reducing work anxiety, and learning a new skill. Specific goals ranged from writing a chapter of a book to listing and selling a house.

These participants were asked to rate their progress and the degree to which they had accomplished their goals. At the end of the study, the individuals in Group 1 only accomplished 43 percent of their stated goals. Those in Group 4 accomplished 64 percent of their stated goals, while those in Group 5 were the most successful, with an average 76 percent of their goals accomplished.

"My study provides empirical evidence for the effectiveness of three coaching tools: accountability, commitment, and writing down one's goals," Matthews said.

"Nothing can stop the man with the right mental attitude from achieving his goal; nothing on earth can help the man with the wrong mental attitude."

Thomas Jefferson

The Target is Your Ultimate Compelling Outcome

The way that you create a compelling outcome is that you create a scene in the future of exactly what you look like, what you're wearing, what you're doing, and how you are feeling. This is your target.

SMART goals are a fabulous way of creating a compelling outcome.

SMART goals must follow these rules and need to be:

Specific

Measurable

Attainable

Realistic

Timely

For instance, in the example I used previously with Crystal, rather than having a goal that reads: "My goal is to lose weight", which sounds like a tedious task, she would create a compelling scene in the future where she could visualise herself as healthy and fit with her grown-up grandchildren. That's where the heartstrings are pulled.

It's important to find a 'why' so there is an emotional connection, not just a conscious justification.

People typically move away from pain and towards pleasure. Losing weight and exercising might seem like pain to Crystal, but being healthy and fit with her grandchild is now associated with pleasure. Now there's a compelling, motivating reason to achieve that goal.

A vision board is another wonderful way of manifesting your compelling outcome. Vision boards serve as a tool to keep you inspired, keep you on track and keep you motivated.

You may think that vision boards are not for you. Any resource or tool that you can use to manifest your goal can only be helpful. Symbols, pictures, screensavers or automated messages that pop up on your phone would be a great idea.

When I first created a goal for myself to go to Paris with my family, I created a daily reminder that popped up on my phone and said, "I am in beautiful Paris with Jon and Peter and loving every moment."

At the time that I had written this reminder, I had no idea how this trip could be funded. Within 12 months of visualising that goal and constantly seeing that daily reminder pop up, my husband and our two children had the most amazing week in Paris.

Dean's SMART GOAL

One of my clients, Dean, set himself a goal of being a CEO by the age of 30, and by 30 he achieved his goal. When he came to see me, he was 55 and was at a loss as to what else he wanted in life.

After that goal was achieved, he had not set any more goals. I asked him to think about what else he wanted from life and his first reaction was that he didn't know.

After further questioning, he said that he wanted to work in some capacity in a not-for-profit organisation and he wanted to contribute to society in some way. He's now taking steps towards this goal and has saved a picture of a non-profit organisation that he would like to work in as a screensaver on his PC.

He now has a visual reminder of what he wants. He will now notice opportunities and possible connections with other people that may assist with his endeavours. As he was previously not consciously aware of what he wanted, he would have not spotted opportunities if they had arisen. Now he will. His goal is now front of mind, so he will be more likely to take action to get connected to people who will help him move closer to his goal.

Jake's SMART Goal

Jake is a successful Property Sales Manager and was extremely overweight when he first came to see me. Jake enjoyed his food and his wine immensely. He actually loved spending time at home with his family and his life-work balance was quite good, but he didn't have a compelling outcome as to what he specifically wanted.

Together we crafted a compelling outcome, as he needed to know beyond doubt what he was aiming for.

Jake wanted two outcomes:

1. Jake wanted his wife to be sexually attracted to him, as he felt embarrassed about being overweight and having 'man boobs'.

2. Jake wanted his workmates to treat him with respect because he felt that he wasn't respected due to his sloppy appearance.

In the Property Industry, there are regular conventions where people from all over Australia get together, and it is considered important to look successful and attractive.

We created a visualisation of Jake hosting a Christmas function.

In this visualisation, we created a very clear picture of Jake welcoming all his guests from around Australia. He wore a smart new tight shirt. He looked trim, taut, and terrific.

As people were coming through the door, they would exclaim, "Wow, you look amazing!"

He visualised this scene every day and this helped him have an overwhelming emotion, which drove him to do whatever he had to do to achieve this goal.

That exact picture became reality for Jake at that Christmas function.

Jake looked younger than ever before and he was very

proud to be greeting all his guests as they entered the room. He felt in control, confident, and wonderful.

Power Points – Chapter 8

1. Make your goal a target of your energy.

2. Focus on what you want – not what you don't want.

3. Associate your goal with pleasurable and happy feelings.

4. Have a compelling reason to motivate you.

5. Create SMART goals to strive for.

6. Use symbols, pictures, vision boards or other visual reminders to keep you motivated towards your goal and to keep it in the front of your mind.

MD ACTION 8

What I would like you to do is to create a vision board. There are no real rules when it comes to creating a visual interpretation of your hopes and dreams. This is why everyone's board is different. I want you to find a quiet place where you can relax and dream.

8 Target Practice

Permit yourself to dream without your conscious mind intruding on the process. Don't concern yourself with the logistics of getting there at this point.

Allow your mind to wonder into the most inspired future that you can visualise for yourself.

Ask yourself the following questions:

What am I doing?

What am I wearing?

What do I look like?

Who am I surrounded by?

Where do I live?

What do I do for work?

Who are my mentors?

How much money am I earning?

How am I feeling?

How do I want my life to look?

What do I want to do?

What do I want to have?

Then go ahead and find images, words, quotes, and affirmations that remind you of all the images that you see: all of those people you want to meet and be around; the places you want to visit; the events you want to experience; the accomplishments you want to attain; the feelings you want to emulate; and the emotions you want to fill yourself with.

All you need to do is buy a corkboard and just pin or stick your images to it. Or you can just do this virtually and set this as a screensaver or a file on your computer.

This is your target and your vision board will constantly remind you of where you want to go. It reminds you of your compelling outcome so that you can take the necessary actions to get there.

The vision board is DYNAMIC!

You can add or subtract at any time.

Make your most important targets more prominent.

9

Eat Like You Mean It

"The way you think, the way you behave, the way you eat, can influence your life by 30 to 50 years."

Deepak Chopra

Now that you have left your limiting beliefs behind, you are ready to make the necessary changes so that you can achieve your goals.

I'm going to show you how to obtain the dominant mindset you need to be in control of your food choices.

The magic key is:

Discipline without Deprivation

Make smart choices. Take a disciplined approach. Have a strategy but never, ever, feel deprived.

If you feel like you're deprived or on a diet, there is a constant struggle, which at some point will come to an end.

The key is to implement changes with a strategic approach so that the changes will be long-lasting.

I will be sharing proven strategies that can be implemented immediately at family lunches, at meetings and at grand events, so that eating well is inclusive of the way that you live your life.

In Australia, 70% of males and 56% of females are overweight. By 2025, it is estimated that 80% of all Australians will be overweight or obese (2007–08 Australian Bureau of Statistics (ABS) National Health Survey (NHS).

There are very compelling reasons as to why Australians and the rest of the world need to make some major changes to their lifestyles.

In this chapter, I will be sharing knowledge about hidden nasties and unnecessary calories that can easily be avoided by making better choices without affecting how much you enjoy your food.

If you continue to eat the same amount of food that you are eating right now and continue to do little or no exercise, you will gain half a kilo every year.

That's the good news – more than likely, you will eat more and gain more!

This will have a dramatic impact on your health, as you place yourself at risk of getting diabetes, high blood pressure, and other obesity-related illnesses.

When you do make life-lasting changes, you will be feeling fit, healthy, and strong, and your clothes will be fitting you comfortably. You will be full of energy and vitality and making the most of your life by living it to the fullest. You will be there to support your children (if you have any) and then, eventually, any grandchildren.

Your appearance will reflect your inner and outer confidence and success. You are a successful person, so now you need to look the part.

Mistake #1: Skipping Meals

One of the biggest mistakes that overweight people make is that they tend to skip meals – and it's usually breakfast or lunch. This has the effect of plummeting blood-glucose levels, which leads to insulin production, excessive hunger and cravings for sugar and carbohydrates later on in the day.

The cycle looks like this:

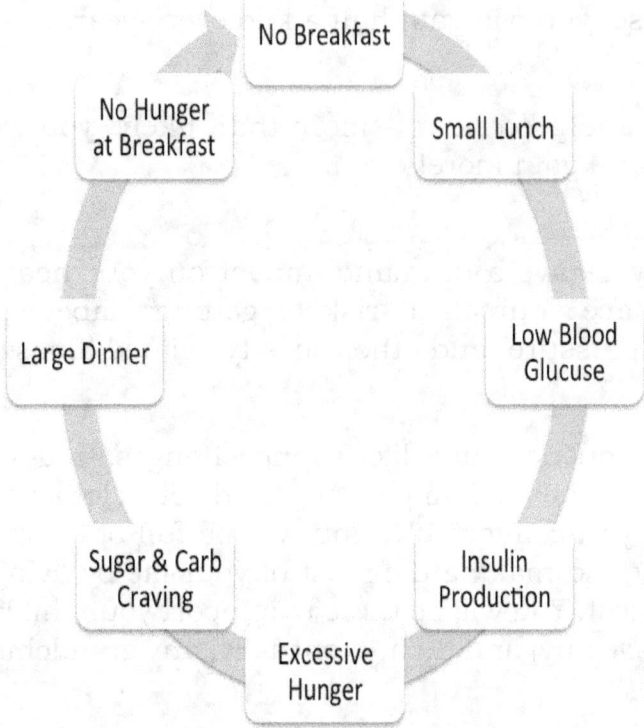

As you can see from the above cycle, when a big meal is eaten the previous evening, you very likely will not be hungry in the morning.

Think of your body as a car where it needs its energy source at the beginning of the day before it sets off on its big day out and uses that petrol progressively throughout the day. At the end of the day, the car is parked in the car park and has no use for further fuel.

Your body is like that car; it needs the most fuel in the morning and less and less as the day progresses. Your body also needs to receive that signal in the morning that it is not starving and there's no need to store fat reserves.

Give yourself time for a delicious, nutritional breakfast. Once you begin to take that first mouthful, a signal is sent to your body that the fast is over and that you are not starving. This way, you will have the energy to do whatever it is that you need to do during your day rather than seeking an energy boost at some point during the day.

By eating consistently throughout the day, at 3–4 hour intervals, the sugar levels will be balanced out so that they don't drop suddenly – which would result in craving the types of foods that your body does not need.

Mistake # 2: Your Food Choices!

The second major mistake that many people make is their food choices when they eat out.

Remember, you always have a choice, no matter where you are!

Food Choices	
Don't Choose	Choose This Instead
Fried foods including chips!	Steamed, grilled or baked foods
Creamy sauces	Tomato based sauces
Creamy dressings	Ask for dressing on the side
Bread	Skip it!
Anything white e.g. white bread, white pasta, white rice	Choose colours of the rainbow instead e.g. greens, reds, yellows
Soft drink	Sparkling mineral water
Butter & cheese	Skip it!
Alcohol & dessert	Limit to special occasions

"The food you eat can be either the safest and most powerful form of medicine or the slowest form of poison."

Ann Wigmore

Fried Food

You think that a few fried chips here and there don't make a difference, but all that saturated fat adds up one week after another and goes straight to your midriff.

Going out for lunch doesn't mean that you have to make bad choices. As a guide, keep away from fried food. It clogs your arteries and it gives you thousands more calories than you actually need for your daily requirements.

Quite often the menu does not stipulate that the item is fried. Always ask! You might read a menu item that reads 'Calamari Salad'. Ask whether the calamari is grilled or fried.

Cream

Keep away from creamy dressings.

I can't tell you the amount of times where the dressing sounded healthy from the menu description and then, when my food arrived, it was covered in a fattening creamy sauce that was nothing like the original description.

Always ask for dressing on the side – even when you think the dressing is low fat. This way, you are in control of exactly how much you put into your mouth and you don't risk your food being smeared with hidden calories.

As for sauces, keep away from creamy sauces such as Carbonara or Alfredo sauces and choose tomato-based sauces like Napolitana instead.

Bread
Don't have any bread before your meal, even if it's sitting on the table right in front of you.

Save your appetite for real food.

Anything White
White potatoes, white rice, and white bread are foods that provide no nutritional benefit, so just avoid them altogether. Choose lean meat, seafood or vegetables.

Soft Drink
Anything that you drink that is NOT water must be regarded as part of your daily food intake. Calories add up a lot quicker when you drink them. One glass of orange juice is like eating 5 oranges!

Butter and Cheese
Butter and cheese is loaded with saturated fat. If you really want to have it, only have this type of food on special occasions.

Alcohol

Have a nice, sparkling natural mineral water instead. Or some tap water. Plan the day of the week that you will allow yourself to drink alcohol and only have alcohol on the day that you have pre-selected!

Dessert

Skip It! To be eaten at special events only.

Special Events

Going to a special event does not automatically mean that you eat everything in sight.

Going out to conferences, family dinners, work functions, or Friday night drinks is another contributing factor to you carrying a lot more weight than you should be. It's very tempting to snack on finger food and drink alcohol when it's free flowing, but you need to slow down and take control. Rather than picking and snacking on the various culinary delights, turn your attention to the conversation. Focus on creating or maintaining valuable connections with your friends, associates or colleagues.

Conscious Eating

An online study in the journal *Personality and Social Psychology Bulletin* (*PSPB*) shows that you are likely to eat much more inferior food when engaging in mindless eating.

Mindless eating is easy to do when at a special event, as the focus is usually the conversation rather than what you are choosing to put on your plate. With finger food, one usually has no idea how much is actually being consumed. Get a plate and choose carefully and then sit down to eat. Engaging in mindless eating at special events, family dinners, conferences, and work functions would be okay if they were held irregularly, but they can be a consistent fixture in your calendar.

There always seems to be something going on at work, some celebration, some gathering, and some meeting where there are platters of food. There are certain types of foods that are served at these events that simply should not be consumed on a regular basis. Many people who come to see me have multiple excuses as to why they can't implement the strategies that I suggest to them. A typical excuse is that they do not have a choice as to what they're going to eat if they are at a special event or work conference, because there are no healthy options.

This is simply not true. You have total control over everything you choose to put into your mouth. I worked in the corporate world for 22 years and I attended a lot of conferences and off-site workshops. The key is to specify your dietary requirements to the Event Organiser before the date. And those requirements might be a request for something as simple as "no fried food". Your needs will be catered for and you will get healthier choices.

Dinners with Multiple Courses

If you are attending dinners on a regular basis, you need to avoid having multiple courses. Multiple courses on a regular basis are way too much food. Your stomach isn't that big. You don't need to eat that much food and, if you do eat that much food, your stomach's going to continually expand and be capable of storing a lot more.

Others often say that, at the end of a long day at work, they feel like they 'deserve' to relax with their team and enjoy some good food and wine. You can relax and enjoy yourself and make wise food choices at the same time. Once you start to make wiser food choices, you will be surprised as to how easy it is to make permanent changes in the way you choose your food. Food is not a reward; it's simply an energy source.

Stop seeing food as a reward when it's NOT. Food is an energy source and alcohol is a poison ... but more on that later!

Power Points – Chapter 9
1. Discipline without deprivation is the key to healthy eating.

2. You can eliminate unhealthy or empty calories by making conscious food choices.

3. Eating out doesn't mean you have to stray from healthy eating.

4. Work-related functions like conferences and meetings shouldn't cause you to go off your healthy eating plan.

5. You are the one who is in control of what you eat and drink.

6. Some advance planning on your part can eliminate problems with finding healthy food choices at special events.

MD ACTION 9

Plan and schedule your week in relation to food and exercise just as you would your work week.

Work out exactly what time you need to wake up so that you can take your time in eating a nutritious breakfast.

Plan your week and decide which day is your "cheat" day – the day you will have a bit more than usual and perhaps some alcohol so that you do not feel like you are deprived or on a diet.

Mindset Dominance

your weekly menu & exercise planner

Ready for a healthy new you? Create a chart like this, print this chart, and use it to plan your meals, snacks and exercise. remember to enjoy two to three treats a week so you feel confident about keeping it up. if your 'what i actually ate' columns don't tally with what you'd planned it up.

		Breakfast			Lunch			Dinner			Snacks			Exercise
	Planned													
SUN	Actual													
	What I was feeling at the time													
	Planned													
MON	Actual													
	What I was feeling at the time													
	Planned													
TUE	Actual													
	What I was feeling at the time													
	Planned													
WED	Actual													
	What I was feeling at the time													
	Planned													
THU	Actual													
	What I was feeling at the time													
	Planned													
FRI	Actual													
	What I was feeling at the time													
	Planned													
SAT	Actual													
	What I was feeling at the time													

10

Booze Buster

"I made a commitment to completely cut out drinking and anything that might hamper me from getting my mind and body together. And the floodgates of goodness have opened upon me, spiritually and financially."

Denzel Washington

If you consistently drink alcohol as part of your weekly routine, then this chapter is for you. If you're consuming unnecessary calories and you find it difficult to lose weight, read on.

Apart from making smarter food choices, the other crucial part of the equation for busy people is the amount of booze that is being consumed. Alcohol is very fattening, so apart from the calories that you are drinking, the fact is that you are likely to eat more when you're drinking as the ability to make smart choices diminishes.

A standard glass of wine can contain as many calories as a piece of chocolate, and a pint of lager has about the same calorie count as a packet of chips. The average wine drinker in Australia takes in around 3,448 calories from alcohol every single month! Drinking 5 pints of beer in a week adds up to 44,200 calories over a year, which is equivalent to eating 221 doughnuts! And many drinkers add to their calorie count by having snacks such as chips, nuts, or finger food to accompany their drink.

To make things worse, a heavy drinking session is often followed by an unhealthy breakfast to help cope with the hangover, which again helps to pile on all those extra kilos.

The drinking habits of busy people probably started many years ago, when they were much younger. Perhaps they were exercising a lot more. So, even though they would be catching up for regular drinking sessions at the pub with their mates, they were probably more active and their metabolisms were fired up.

As they got older and busier, they continued to drink the same amount of calories and eat the same types of food, but their energy expenditure dramatically decreased, so there was a surplus of calories, which usually went straight to their bellies.

Apart from the fact that alcohol is so fattening, it is also a poisonous drug and each time you drink it, you are poisoning your body little by little. In fact, if you drink a small amount of pure alcohol, it can actually kill you. This means that it is a poison. It affects every major organ in the body. Alcohol causes cancers, cirrhosis of the liver, and may shorten your life considerably.

There are two distinct camps within the scientific community about the effect of moderate alcohol consumption on longevity, as the evidence of health benefits are conflicting. The bottom line is that you are fooling yourself if you actually believe you are drinking alcohol for health benefits. If you want to reduce your risk of heart disease, there are many, many other things you can do besides turn to alcohol such as exercise or improving your diet.

One in eight deaths of Australians who are under 25 are caused to some extent by alcohol consumption (usually by misadventure). Alcohol is second only to tobacco as a preventable cause of drug-related death and hospitalisation, and costs our community in excess of $15 billion every year.

Some Alcohol Facts – Australia (Australian Bureau of Statistics 2012)
One in five adults consume more than two standard drinks per day on average. This level of consumption is associated with a lifetime risk of harm from alcohol-related disease or injury.

Drinking rates are higher among older Australian adults than younger Australians.

Harmful consumption of alcohol is associated with estimated social and economic costs to the Australian community in excess of $15 billion annually.

What will your compelling reason be to reduce your consumption of alcohol?

Alcohol debilitates your immune system and systematically destroys your nervous system. Alcohol deadens your senses one by one and impedes your concentration.

Chronic drinkers are more liable to contract diseases like pneumonia and tuberculosis than people who do not drink too much. Drinking a lot on a single occasion slows your body's ability to ward off infections – even up to 24 hours after getting drunk (National Institute of Alcohol Abuse and Alcoholism, Australia).

Many people have the misconception that alcohol quenches their thirst, but that is simply a misperception. Alcohol exacerbates thirst and is a natural diuretic. Alcohol causes cells to shrink, which has the effect of depleting the body's natural water stores.

Think about how you feel when you have been drinking – your mouth during the night is likely to feel dry and parched and you wake up very thirsty.

If you don't lower your alcohol intake, you'll continue to feel lethargic and remain overweight. Just think about who you are likely to see nursing a glass of beer – the person with the beer belly or the person with the six pack?

Apart from alcohol being a poisonous substance, it is a high-calorie, sugar-laden drink. Have a look at the quick reference guide below so you can see how many calories there are in typical drinks.

Alcohol & Calories		
Alcoholic Drink (alcohol content)	Serving Size	Calories
Red Wine (13.5%)	150 ml	100 - 120
White Wine (11.5%)	150 ml	70 - 120
Sparkling Wine (11.5%)	150 ml	70 - 120
Cider (4.7%)	200 ml	75
Full Strength Beer (4.8%)	425 ml Schooner	155
Premix Gin & Tonic (4.5%)	375 ml Can	320
Vodka & Soda (4.0%)	30 ml Spirit + 150ml Soda	64
Premix Rum & Cola (4.6%)	375 ml Can	248
Gin & Tonic (4.5%)	30 ml Spirit + 150ml Tonic	200
Pina Colada (13%)	150 ml	290 - 480

"First you take a drink, then the drink takes a drink, and then the drink takes you."

F. Scott Fitzgerald

Small changes can lead to big results.

Training Time Required to Burn Off the Calories from Alcohol (minutes)				
Alcoholic Drink	Walking	Swimming	Running	Cycling
Beer 355 ml	30	17	12	13
Light Beer 355ml	20	11	8	9
Low Carb Beer 355ml	23	13	9	10
White Wine 200ml	29	16	12	13
Red Wine 200ml	28	16	11	12
Spirits 30ml (no mixer)	13	7	5	6

A Beer in the Hand – Gary

Many people don't consider how fattening their drinks really are. One of my clients, Gary, came to me for weight loss, and he really could not understand why he wasn't losing weight as he was eating what he thought were healthy meals at regular times. But what we found was that Gary was drinking four glasses of beer for most nights of the week. This was an additional whopping 3,100 calories every single week from the beer alone. As soon as we created more alcohol-free days for Gary, as well as having fewer glasses on the days when he was having them, the weight just started to drop off.

For the Love of Wine – Steve

One of my clients, Steve, created a much-loved routine where he would pour himself a glass of wine the moment that he got home from work. He loved putting the music on, which he would have in the background as he poured his first glass of wine as he was preparing dinner. Steve considered himself to be an excellent cook and a bit of a wine buff, and he proceeded to drink half the bottle of wine, even before he was ready to eat his dinner!

As Steve was not prepared to stop drinking his beloved red wine, we created a strategy where he delayed opening the bottle until dinner was served. This tiny change alone resulted in Steve drinking half the amount that he was previously drinking! This had an immediate impact on his health, wellbeing, and his waistline.

You Never Know What You Will Get Dealt – Sue

One of my clients, Sue, would go to the neighbours' house every Sunday evening for a game of cards. She would take a bottle of wine with her and consume it during the course of the evening. When I suggested that she swap the bottle of wine for a bottle of sparkling natural mineral water, her immediate reaction was that she couldn't do that, as it wouldn't be sociable or appropriate.

Sue's belief that she couldn't possibly take natural mineral water with her instead of a bottle of wine was completely unfounded and simply not true.

One year down the track and Sue is still going to her card night with her sparkling natural mineral water; people were initially a bit surprised but, at the end of the day, no one really cared about whether she drank wine or natural mineral water. Sue has now lost all the excess weight that she was previously carrying and is feeling fantastic.

Strategy!

Step 1

The first step is to monitor and record your actual alcohol intake by drinking one standard glass at a time. A standard glass of wine is 100 ml – not 150 ml, as is served at most restaurants and pubs.

An easy way of doing this is to place an elastic band around a glass after measuring 100 ml and only pour your wine up to that point where the elastic band is.

Many clients are shocked to see the number of standard glasses that they were actually drinking over the course of one week. It is very important to be consciously aware of our behaviours so that we can change them.

Step 2

Have a glass of water in between each glass of alcohol. This slows down the consumption of alcohol and flushes out some of the toxins consumed from the alcohol as well. Whether you feel like it or not, just drink a glass of water instead.

I love drinking a glass of sparkling natural mineral water between alcoholic drinks. It helps me feel that I am in control of my alcohol consumption and I always find that after a certain point I cease wanting any more alcohol, whereas if I don't use this strategy, I'm more likely to drink more as my frontal lobe, which determines future consequences based on current actions, is not operating at its optimal capacity.

Step 3

Become accountable!

How Accountability Works

It was the 31st of December, 2010, and I had had an exhausting month, so I was looking forward to relaxing and letting my hair down for a New Year's Eve party that we were invited to at our friend's beach house.

My golden rule regarding alcohol is that I don't have shots, as I do not want concentrated alcohol entering my blood stream at a rapid rate.

On this particular evening, I broke my golden rule! After drinking a few glasses of champagne, my judgement became blurred; when our host brought out the Black Sambuca, I decided to have one, and then one shot of Sambuca inevitably led to another, and I am embarrassed to admit that I do not even know how many shots I had! This resulted in a rather terrible evening where I got drunk and I had to endure the most torturous hangover the next day.

So I gave myself the usual oath:

"I am NEVER going to drink again!"

A few days later, I decided to change this to:

"I am not going to drink for 100 days!"

I felt like I needed to cleanse my body and clear out the toxins by not drinking for 100 days.

I was fearful that my new resolution would fail if I was to attend a party where I thought I would be at my weakest. I hoped that I wouldn't be going to any parties so that I wouldn't be tempted to drink.

True to form, whenever we make a resolution, the Universe has a way of putting it to the test almost immediately! One of my sisters decided to hold an ad hoc party within two days of my resolution and, sure enough, as I walked into her house, she told me to go and pour myself a glass of champagne. Instead of telling her about my resolution not to drink, I said "I'll have some later." Later on, she came to me again and said, "You still haven't got yourself a glass of champagne!" I told her that I would have it later. Why didn't I tell her about my resolution? Was it because I thought I might weaken and have some? Probably!

When we sat down to eat, she came and placed a glass of Veuve Clicquot right in front of me. So I drank it! And I drank another as well. I didn't enjoy the taste of either of them. I felt that I simply could not say "No"! My thinking was, "When would I have the opportunity to have Veuve again?" The truth is, I could have it whenever I wanted to, but the perception I had was that I would be missing out if I didn't have it right now!

I knew that I had to make myself accountable.

The moment I arrived home from that party, I posted a status on Facebook that read "I will not drink any alcohol for 100 days!" I knew that everyone who I could possibly drink with was on Facebook, so once I made that statement, I knew that I had total accountability. In fact, when the 100 days arrived, I was finding it so natural not to drink that I went for an extra 10 days.

My biggest revelation during that time was that I enjoyed get-togethers, parties and functions even more. That was the biggest "a-ha" moment. I was able to concentrate on conversation and focus on other people. I didn't have to worry about whether I had a drink, whether I was eating, or whatever. I was purely focused on connecting with other people and enjoying their company.

That helped me understand that the thought that I needed to drink at parties was absolute and complete BS. That wasn't the case at all. I enjoyed parties better without the alcohol.

If you feel that you can't enjoy yourself at a party or a get-together without having a glass of alcohol, do it once to experience whether that is actually true or not. Tell yourself that you can do it. When you have done it once, you have then proven to yourself that you can do it, and then it gets easier each and every time.

Power Points – Chapter 10
1. Alcohol consumption keeps us from reaching our weight loss goals. Not only do we gain weight from the booze, but also poor food choices are made when our decision-making is not at its best.

2. Alcohol contains hidden calories that pack on the kilos and is toxic to our bodies.

3. Having even a few AFDs will bring a positive result.

4. Not drinking allows you true interactions and enjoyment of the people around you.

5. Making yourself accountable for giving up alcohol will strengthen your resolve and garner support from friends and loved ones.

MD ACTION 10

Make yourself accountable with alcohol.

Give it up or moderate your alcohol intake.

Who are you going to tell?

It is imperative that you do not avoid social get-togethers. Go to all the events that you would normally go to but experience them without alcohol. You may be surprised to find out that it's a lot easier than you thought it was going to be. You have created a brand new neural pathway where you are able to attend a party, dinner, function or whatever and have a great time without alcohol!

11

Non-negotiables

"I do have high standards. I look at everything I have done and think, 'Why wasn't that better?' Part of my motivation is from crippling self-doubt – I have got to prove myself wrong."

Michael Palin

Non-negotiables are those rules that you consistently adhere to, which keep you aligned with attaining your goals and living your life on your terms. You live by these high standards no matter what the events and circumstances of your life. You do not waver.

Consistency is a vital key to delivering results.

Anybody can go to the gym once every couple of months, or anybody can go for a walk when they feel like it, but that's not going to get them the results they want.

What gets results is when you set yourself up with non-negotiable guidelines that you consistently stick to.

- There's no thinking.

- There's no deciding about whether you will do something.

- There are no ifs or buts. You just know you have to do it.

- You run your life rather than your life running you. You take control of your life. This is all about keeping high standards and getting results because of them.

"Non-Negotiables" at Work

If you are successful at work, it is very likely that you already have set yourself high standards in your work life and that's why you are reaping the rewards there. Wherever you have non-negotiable rules, wherever you have high standards and guidelines, that's where you get consistent results.

What are those high standards that are keeping you successful at work?

Do you ensure that deadlines are always met irrespective of time constraints at work?

Are you organised?

Do you plan your schedule so that everything gets done in order of priority?

Do you consistently add more value than is requested of you?

Compare these work guidelines to those you have for your personal goals.

When you don't have those high standards in your personal life, that's where your health suffers.

How to Create Non-Negotiable Standards

Non-Negotiable #1 – Get Aligned to Your Values
Non-negotiable standards need to be aligned to your values and your goals, not other people's goals for you.

Non-Negotiable #2 – Exercise 6 Out of 7 Days
Exercise MUST be a non-negotiable daily activity, if your goal is to be fit and healthy. You simply cannot be fit without exercise. If you think that you can be lean, fit, and healthy without consistent exercise, you are fooling yourself.

You may lose weight for a period of time if you maintain good, healthy, eating habits but, after a while, the weight's going to pile back on. It's going to be way too hard to consistently eat the quantity of food you need to eat to maintain your weight loss without the benefit of exercise. As we get older and our metabolism slows down, the primary way to keep that weight off is to consistently exercise.

My recommendation is that exercise needs to be scheduled every day for 6 out of 7 days per week, no matter where you are and what you're doing. There are varied opinions on the frequency and intensity of exercise, but if you do not plan to do it regularly, you will not create the necessary habit. There is simply no excuse.

Negotiating With Your Inner CEO – Andrew
One of my clients, Andrew, is a CEO of a large company, and he agreed to exercise regularly.

At the very next session, I asked Andrew how his exercise sessions went since the last time I had seen him. He replied by admitting that he did not exercise at all as he was "too busy at work". So then we talked it through and what we found is that he failed to prioritise his health before the needs of his business, a habit he has done for many years.

When we examined the details of the circumstances, he reluctantly admitted that the business would not have suffered if he took time out to exercise. All he needed to do was spend a few minutes planning *how* he could fit his exercise in his daily routine. A seemingly impossible problem was solved with a simple solution.

Planning

When I was working as a Senior Project Manager for Australia's largest service provider, I implemented strategy and delivery of business and technology projects in major companies. I blocked out a 90-minute lunch break in my calendar as a daily activity, so that no one could book a meeting during that time. Those 90 minutes gave me enough time to train, shower and eat my lunch with 10 minutes to spare.

On rare occasions, I would miss out on my scheduled midday exercise session due to some urgent meeting. I would always make sure that I would make up for that missed session at some point, whether it was before or after work. A day never went by without my 'non-negotiable' activity of daily exercise where I moved my body with enough intensity so that I was sweating and feeling invigorated for the day ahead.

Work Retreats and Exercise

In fact, exercise is such a non-negotiable for me that, no matter where I am, no matter what I'm doing, I do it. Even if I have to go away for a work retreat, I always make sure that I take my runners and my training gear. When I arrive at the retreat, the very first thing that I do is ask other people that are at the retreat with me, "Who wants to have a run tomorrow morning?"

You would be surprised that there is always at least one other person who has my values and agrees. This provides me with accountability and gives me the opportunity to become connected to someone at a completely different level and I have a brand new experience. At that time in the morning, when everything is so still, it's just the most beautiful time to go out for a run.

Special Events and Exercise

Even on special events, like Christmas Day, I will still organise to go for a run the day after Christmas Day with someone else (to make sure that I actually go). I know that I would have consumed a hell of a lot more calories than my body actually needed on Christmas Day and it gave me time to burn those suckers off!

In fact, whenever I overindulge on one day, it is even more important to even out the balance and feel better about myself. If I was overeating or drinking at a special occasion or a party, the last thing I want to do is sleep in the next day and feel sluggish and lethargic because I haven't bothered to move my body sufficiently that morning.

Plane Trips and Exercise

No matter where you are and what you are doing, there is absolutely no excuse not to move. When I went on a long haul plane trip overseas recently, I made the effort to do some stretches and squats so that I at least had the blood flowing through my body. This is also great for lowering any risk of Deep Vein Thrombosis.

I was not going to just sit in a seat for several hours just because I was in an aeroplane.

You have to constantly be thinking about what you want to do with your body. Get that blood flowing and those calories burning so you can feel good about yourself and keep your non-negotiable contract with yourself.

Non-Negotiable # 3 – Keep Away From Deep Fried Food!

A non-negotiable if you want to stay fit and fabulous is to keep deep fried foods to an absolute minimum and to be eaten only on rare occasions, if at all. Fried foods are the bad guys. Deep fried food is dripping with saturated fat, clogs your arteries, and piles on those calories.

In 2006, I attended a New Year's Eve party at a popular venue where about 90% of the finger food that was served up that evening was fried. I did not consume a single item that was deep-fried.

The next day I wrote in my achievements journal, which captures my magical moments and achievements.

"01.01.2006 – I am so proud that I am no longer that person that eats fried food."

This was a wonderful way of reinforcing to myself that no matter where I am and what's happening around me, I am just not going to eat fried food.

Another time, I went to a family christening where I was served all the foods that I would prefer not to eat and I literally did not eat anything from the venue. I had decided that I am not the kind of person that eats fried food. It did not matter how hungry I was. I simply was not going to eat any. No different to a vegetarian who attends an event where only meat is served – they are unlikely to make an exception and eat meat on that occasion. Instead, I went to the nearest cafe and bought some rice paper rolls, which kept me satisfied until I got home.

TIP – Take some snacks with you if you think there may be an "unhealthy food alert" or speak to the event organiser beforehand and let them know your dietary requirements.

There was one point in my life when I did eat those foods and did enjoy them. Once you stop eating them and you see them for the pockets of fat that they really are, you just don't want to be putting that food into your mouth and that fat on to your belly anymore. It is simply not worth it. You find that you start to become repulsed at these types of fatty foods as your perception changes.

Non-Negotiable # 4 – No Missed Meals When Hungry!
It is vital that you keep your sugar levels stable throughout the day, so making time for meals , if you are hungry, is a must.

When you do not have meals at regular intervals or you have foods that have a high GI (glycaemic index) rating, your sugar levels quickly drop soon afterwards.

Your body will crave foods that are high in sugar as your body naturally craves the kinds of foods that will bring your sugar levels back up very quickly.

And these are precisely the types of foods that will send your sugar levels skyrocketing down once again, as the foods are digested quickly and you feel hungry in smaller time intervals.

This leads to a never-ending cycle that is anti-productive to your goals.

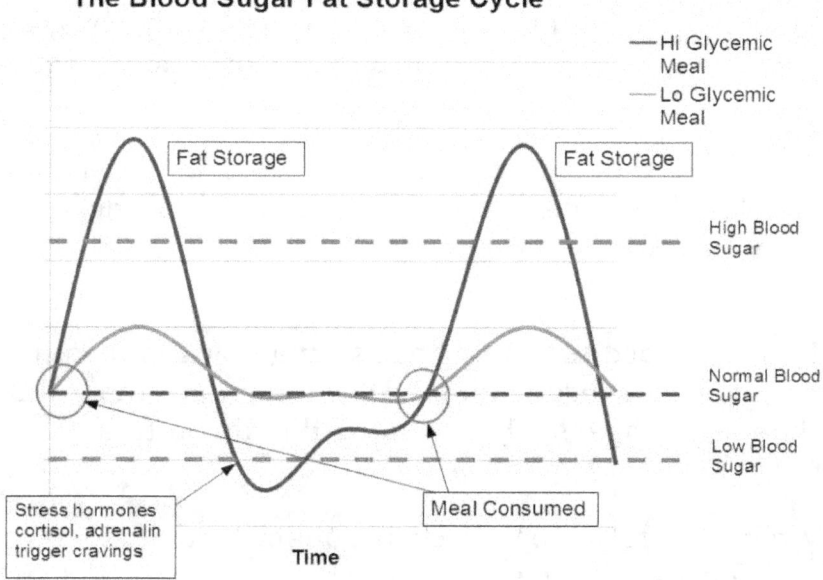

When you eat low GI foods, your body will digest these foods slowly, leaving you feeling full for longer and allowing you to eat less calories without feeling hungry.

"You have competition every day because you set such high standards for yourself that you have to go out every day and live up to that."

Michael Jordan

Too Busy to Eat – Robert

Robert held a high profile job, and on most days his only actual sit-down meal was dinnertime. He believed that he did not have time to eat a proper breakfast or lunch. This meant that Robert's dinner was his biggest meal. This habit was leading to a sluggish metabolism.

We then scheduled regular time slots for breakfast and lunch so that he wasn't excessively hungry by dinnertime.

Robert needed to accept that sitting down and eating regular meals throughout the day is far more important than anything else that he needed to do on that day.

When Robert made it a non-negotiable activity to have a sit-down breakfast and lunch, he scheduled it in his calendar, and all other activities naturally fitted around them.

Robert now makes the time to stop and eat – even if it's only for 20 minutes.

Robert now eats an additional two meals and one afternoon snack every day. He found that he was able to have much smaller meals for dinner and the weight just dropped off.

People who prioritise fitness will adhere to this rule as if their life depended on it. They will take food into meetings if need be, as they will not allow more than 3–4 hours to pass before they have their next meal as they do not want their energy to be sourced from their muscle mass as opposed to their fat stores. When energy is sourced from muscles, lean muscle and strength is adversely affected.

Non-Negotiable # 5 – Protein With Every Meal

Every meal should have a protein component to it.

Proteins are necessary to keep those sugar levels stable throughout the day. This doesn't mean you do not eat carbohydrates – it just means that there must be a protein component in every one of your meals to sustain you throughout the day.

Proteins
Red Meat
- Fillet steak, 100 grams = 20.9 grams of protein

White Meat
- Chicken breast (skinless), 100 grams = 23.5 grams of protein

- Turkey breast (skinless), 100 grams = 22.3 grams of protein

Fish
- Tuna (canned), 100 grams = 26.3 grams of protein

- Orange roughy, 100 grams = 22.6 grams

Eggs and Dairy

- Egg, large = 6 grams protein

- Cottage cheese, ½ cup = 15 grams of protein

- Yoghurt, 1 cup = usually 8–12 grams of protein (check label)

Beans (including soy)

- Tofu, ½ cup = 20 grams of protein

- Soy milk, 1 cup = 6–10 grams of protein

- Most beans (black, pinto, lentils etc. cooked), ½ cup = 7–10 grams of protein

- Soy beans, ½ cup cooked = 14 grams of protein

- Split peas, ½ cup cooked = 8 grams of protein

Nuts and Seeds

- Peanut butter, 2 tablespoons = 8 grams of protein (I prefer Almond Spread from the Health Food Shop)

- Peanuts, Almonds, ¼ cup = 8 grams of protein. It is recommended you do not have more than 10 almonds per day

- Sunflower seeds, ¼ cup = 6 grams of protein

- Pumpkin seeds, ¼ cup = 8 grams of protein

- Flax seeds, ¼ cup = 8 grams of protein

(Source: Better Health Channel – State Government of Victoria)

Non-Negotiable # 6 – Limit Alcohol

There should be at least 5–6 alcohol-free days per week. For strategies on alcohol consumption, you can refer to Chapter 10!

Cheat Meals

What if you don't want to stick to 'non-negotiables' 100% of the time?

That's okay – really, it is. It is the choices that you make on a consistent basis which shape your life and your body.

Remember, it's what you consistently do that matters!

Every now and again, most people want to indulge a little. If you want some more flexibility to adapt to events and circumstances, choose ONE meal in your week that can be classified as a 'cheat meal'.

During this meal, allow yourself to have the foods and drink that you would not normally have – but, do not overindulge. Do not eat until you feel too full or unwell! You want to enjoy the indulgence, not walk away regretting it.

The way that a 'cheat' meal works is that you choose a pre-determined date and time where you will have that little bit extra. For instance, if you know that there's a party coming up, or a special event, lunch or dinner, you can choose to have your cheat meal at that event.

If you have a number of special events in the same week, choose only one where you allow yourself to cheat. Remember, if you cheat beyond this day, you are only cheating yourself!

You should not overindulge at all of these events. You have to look ahead and decide which day it is going to be. Which will be your "special event" of choice? Which is the day you want to have a bit more food or a bit more discretion in terms of what you're eating? You decide in advance and know that, if you want to be fit and fabulous, you cannot have whatever you want every time you want it! There is a price and a payoff for everything!

Power Points – Chapter 11

1. You set high standards and have non-negotiables in your work life. You need to have them in your personal life around your workout and eating habits as well.

2. You need to set these non-negotiables up for exercise and eating no matter where you happen to be. Adapt to situations away from home, special events or retreats by sticking to your non-negotiable plan and making it work.

3. Keeping off deep fried foods is non-negotiable.

4. You should be eating when hungry to stabilise your blood-glucose levels.

5. Have some protein with every meal.

6. Limit alcohol.

7. Allow yourself one cheat meal a week to have the foods that you wouldn't normally allow yourself or to have a little bit more.

MD ACTION 11

List all your "non-negotiables" that you currently have in your life. These "non-negotiables" are standards that you adhere to.

Relationship "Non-Negotiables" May Be:
"I will speak to my mother once a week."

"Date night with my wife is once a fortnight."

"I will spend quality time with the kids every Sunday."

Work "Non-Negotiables" May Be:
"All tasks will be submitted by the due date, as I never submit anything late."

Make sure you also include a list of "non-negotiables" for your health and wellbeing. So, apart from the ones that I have suggested, I want you to write your own "non-negotiable" list.

What do you absolutely refuse to budge on?

What will you make non-negotiable? How are you going to live your life from now on so that you can achieve the outcome that you want?

When you live by guidelines that are aligned with your values, there is less chance of having regrets; you can be fit, healthy and achieve your goals.

12

Forever Fit

"Your beliefs become your thoughts, your thoughts become your words, your words become your actions, your actions become your habits, your habits become your values, and your values become your destiny."

Mahatma Gandhi

There's no point making any changes in our life if they're going to be temporary. Why would you?

You have gone to all this trouble of breaking old habits and establishing new ones. You have created new ways of doing things and established new neural pathways, and then suddenly it all comes to a stop and you lose focus, you get distracted, and all the weight comes back on.

This usually occurs because you have tapped into some old, unhelpful neural pathways and you are back to where you started. You feel like a failure because you have gone to all that trouble, and then it seems like you have not made any positive changes at all.

You almost feel embarrassed because people have seen you make changes in your life and then you have reverted back to your old, unhealthy, destructive habits.

It's very important that you take the principles of this book to heart and make permanent changes in your life. This way, you have established brand new lifelong habits that will keep you fit and healthy forever.

You need to get off the diet rollercoaster that's a lifelong battle of being "good" or being "bad". Make the most of your life and make every moment count. If you feel like you are making sacrifices or you feel like you are deprived for a short-term goal, those unhelpful habits will reappear and then you need to start all over again from square one! How frustrating will that be?

Ultimately, you want to be at peace with yourself and the way that you live your life, rather than waging battles to break the latest bad habit.

Staying strong for just 21 days to establish a new habit is actually a myth. Habit formation typically takes longer than that. The best estimation is that it takes 66 days, although the duration of the habit formation is likely to differ depending on who you are and what you are trying to do. So, as long as you continue to do your new healthy habit consistently for around 66 days in any given situation, you have formed a new habit.

If you feel that your changed behaviour is hard work, at some point you are likely to stop struggling and revert back to old habits. You have to be prepared for the fact that a crisis or negative event is bound to happen in your life, and this is the real challenge that you need to overcome. Once you overcome those challenges with your new habits intact, you know you are ready for anything. You are not tested when everything is going well. The true test comes when you are still working it out.

Will you be able to stay on track?

The brain has billions of neural pathways, which were created when habits were formed. New neural pathways are established when the creation of neurons link together in new ways. These new neural pathways are your habits and they become stronger the more they are used. As the new neural habit becomes stronger, the new habit becomes the habit that you default to. However, the old neural pathways will still be there, so if you ever tap into the old neural pathways, it's possible to reignite them again.

If you have established a habit of exercising every day, it will be part of your routine to get up every day and exercise, no matter whether that day is Boxing Day, Christmas Day, or the day after a big party. If that's a new habit that you have established, you are more likely to do it.

A common mistake people make is that they disrupt their routine when circumstances change. For example, they go on a holiday and make a conscious decision to take a break from exercise. Your established neural pathway, which you painstakingly created, will then become weaker once you have interrupted this habit.

How do we make sure that our habits stick?

Habits change permanently when the choices that you make are slow and steady. It is important that you do not feel like you are on a diet or feel deprived. When you do not feel like you are deprived, struggling, or like it's too hard, then there is no reason to revert back to old habits.

If you really want to have something that's fattening or sweet, just have a small amount. Consistency is key to ensuring that any changes are permanent. No matter what the circumstances, the new habits need to continue.

For example, whenever I go on holidays, I find that I can still keep my running routine, no matter where I go. Last year when I went to Europe, I actually came back home as a better runner because I ran more often than when I was at home. The "no excuses" and non-negotiable mindset are vital here.

It is very likely that there is always a good excuse as to why something can't be done, but recognise it as an excuse and always have a backup plan. For example, one of my clients stopped exercising when he travelled with work as he saw exercise as something he would only do when he was at home and his routine was back to normal.

12 Forever Fit

If you are serious about being fit forever, exercise has to be made into a non-negotiable priority so that wherever you are in the world you use the hotel gym, go for a run or whatever. You can go for a run mostly anywhere and anytime so that you start the day invigorated, sharp and alert.

I wasn't always this person who ran. I started running at the age of 38. Up to that point, the people that ran seemed like people from another planet, which I would never visit. I first started running because it is one of the most efficient fat-burning mechanisms there is. I figured that if I ran, I could eat more. It wasn't long before the "Runner's High" got me addicted. The "Runner's High" is where endorphins are released into the brain, which has a biochemical effect as the brain's naturally occurring opiates get into the blood stream.

Studies showed that endorphins are produced during running and attach themselves to areas of the brain associated with emotions, in particular the limbic and prefrontal areas, which are those areas that are activated when people are involved in a romantic love affair.

Researchers in Germany, using advances in neuroscience, have reported that running does elicit a flood of endorphins in the brain (University of Bonn. "The Runner's High: Opioidergic Mechanisms in the Human Brain" are published in the journal *Cerebral Cortex*, 6 March 2008).

Running makes me feel so damn good that I feel that anyone that doesn't get this feeling is really missing out.

It has been proven that endorphins will flood the brain with other forms of intense exercise as well. If running is not for you, as long as the exercise is performed with intensity, these endorphins will be buzzing around your brain too!

Challenge yourself by constantly pushing yourself to the next level. Cardiovascular activity is the easiest and fastest way to burn fat.

"We are what we repeatedly do. Excellence, then, is not an act, but a habit."

Aristotle

Use the following steps as a guide to steadily and gradually increase your cardio fitness. Move on to the next step when the previous step has been established as a consistent routine.

1. Walk slowly for 30 minutes a day.

2. Walk fast for 30 minutes every day.

3. Walk up hills at a fast pace for 30 minutes a day.

4. Introduce jogging by jogging 5 minutes then walking for 10 minutes, and over time gradually increase the distance you can jog and then eventually run.

Once you are doing cardio on a regular basis, you will need to start regular strength training for improved muscular tone, healthy weight, and bone density. You are never too old to start strength training.

Get resourceful!

A personal trainer is a fabulous investment, as their job is to push you beyond your perceived limits safely.

I used to see a personal trainer twice a week for 30 minutes per session for a number of years, and the benefit to my fitness levels was enormous.

Massage
Remedial massage is also a must when you train regularly to keep your body in tune. If you owned a Ferrari, would you keep it in your garage or would you take it to a technician on a regular basis to keep it performing at its peak?

Our bodies are far more complex and valuable than that Ferrari.

Massage has many benefits, both as a preventative strategy and in the treatment of injuries. In general the benefits are:

- Increases blood flow to our muscles, organs, and other tissue

- Helps to flush out toxins stored in our muscles

- Helps to stimulate the lymphatic system

- Restores and improves our range of motion

- Helps to facilitate the repair of musculoskeletal injuries

- Prompts the release of endorphins

- Helps to reduce stress.

Once people start an exercise regime, they may easily get injured due to bad form or too much exercise too soon. This confirms their previously held belief that exercise is just too hard and it stops them in the tracks before they have built any momentum.

Get yourself massaged every fortnight and keep your muscles supple and working at their ultimate potential.

What if you start gaining weight back on that you previously lost?

First of all, it is important to determine whether you have gained back fat or muscle. Muscle is heavier than fat. If you have been doing any form of strength training, it could be that a portion of the weight gain is from increased muscle mass.

I have scales that show me the percentage of my weight attributed to fat and the percentage attributed to fluid. This way, I am comparing apples with apples.

If your weight gain can be attributed to fat, instead of seeing it as a failure, view the weight loss as a mini achievement. You have already created the neural pathways that helped you to lose weight – reconnect with them.

Review your choices and learn what you can do differently next time so that you can implement strategies for the future.

When you reverted back to those old unhelpful behaviours, you tapped back into old neural pathways and reactivated them. All you need to do is tap BACK into the new neural pathways, because at least they are now established and it's easier to tap into them. This means that this time around it will be easier for you to re-establish your good habits.

For example, it will be easier to recommence exercise if, at some point, you have exercised and then stopped as opposed to never having started.

What if a crisis occurs and you start overeating or drinking as a crutch? The simple answer is STOP. Take a step back and get back into your good new habits. This is just a setback to overcome. You can almost be guaranteed that negative events will happen. This is the most important time for you to be vigilant with maintaining your new habits, and you will find that you will become stronger from having had that experience.

This is when it really counts, as your neural pathways will become doubly strong.

Tried, Tested and Passed – Brad

Brad came to me to stop smoking. Almost immediately he had a number of negative events that occurred in his life one after the other. It was bizarre. His wife had a serious car accident, his mother became seriously ill and was rushed to hospital, and it went on and on. During this time, he never considered smoking, and because he got through those negative events without resorting to lighting a single cigarette it confirmed to him without a doubt that no situational circumstance could lead him to ever smoke again.

What if family and friends or colleagues make it difficult for you to stick to your resolve?

Misery loves company. People generally feel uncomfortable with other people's achievements as it leads them to reflect on their own lives. They will subconsciously sabotage your achievements, even when they don't know that they are doing it. It could be that they are offering you that extra can of beer, extra glass of wine, or chocolate bar – because misery loves company.

Calmly and tenderly disregard their negative commentary. Comments like:

"You are losing too much weight" are not really helpful. So just ignore them without being disrespectful. Don't engage, just move on. Understand that, at a subconscious level, misery loves company.

If you are looking fit, taut, and terrific and they are getting larger and looking a lot older than you, then they are likely to feel inadequate in your presence. Your success is showing up their inadequacies, and therefore they will subconsciously do everything that they can in their power to bring you back to where you used to be so that they feel better about themselves.

Don't allow it to happen. Just understand that misery loves company. You are through with misery and you are ready to embrace being fit forever.

Power Points – Chapter 12
1. There's no point in making these hard changes only to revert back to old habits. Stay true to your new habits.

2. You will be tested by a situation or circumstance. Your job is to pass the challenge.

3. If you do have a setback, it's not a failure – unless you go back to your old ways. Get back on track right away and move forward.

4. Keep pushing yourself to achieve even more in your workout routine. Invest in a personal trainer.

5. Get a massage to help you feel good while you're stretching and strengthening your body.

6. Don't let outside detractors pull you off-course. Stay true to your commitment and dedicated to your goals.

MD ACTION 12

Keep an 'Achievements and Magical Moments' journal where you document all the achievements and magical moments in every area of your life. Note it all down so that you can celebrate your successes. Capture your achievements and magical moments and look at them regularly.

Sometimes, in this amazing journey that we call life, we go five steps forward and one step back. When you go one step back, pick up your 'Achievements and Magical Moments' journal and have a look at everything that you've achieved to date.

Include events from your work life and your personal life and just see yourself for the amazing, unique person that you really are.

13

Andrew's Interview

I want to know about where your passion for fitness began. Can you tell me about it?
Since I can remember I've always been obsessed with anything athletic and played most sports growing up. Despite this, I was passionate about playing sport rather than with fitness.

Fitness (achieved through training) was more of a means to an end. When I was around 15, I suffered a very serious wrist injury, which kept me from playing any sport for 12 months. Until then, given the amount of sport I was playing, I never really had to be conscious of what I ate (which was a lot!), given that the majority was being burned off. It's not surprising then that I gained significant weight during this time of inactivity when my diet remained the same.

After a few years of lowered self-esteem caused by my weight gain, I finally decided to act upon the eureka moment I had around working out the relationship between diet and appearance. As it was way before the Google era, I started exploring this phenomenon in a more traditional way by visiting the local library and immersing myself in the realm of diet and nutrition. I began to modify my behaviour accordingly and began to see some positive results, which helped to improve my frame of mind.

What was the first big fitness challenge you ever faced?

I was content with the progress I made until I began to notice the fitness magazines I was using as a motivational and information resource were littered with images of chiselled guys with well-pronounced abdominal muscles or "6-packs". I then took my exercise and diet regime to another level in pursuit of this next "fitness challenge".

After months of toil, for the first time I got to the point of conceding defeat and putting it down to it being due to something out of my control, i.e. "I didn't have the genes for this type of physique".

I pondered this for a while, then decided it was time to take my knowledge to the next level to test my hypothesis. I then enrolled myself into a Certificate 3 & 4 Fitness course, which among other things would cover nutrition, exercise prescription, anatomy, and physiology. Completing this course gave me the qualification to become a personal trainer, but my intent was purely to take my own fitness to the next level.

Was there a point where there was a shift in your belief system about what you were physically capable of? Tell me about it.

When I managed to finally create the elusive "6-pack", it made me realise the power of knowledge and science with respect to physical capability. The reality was that I wasn't working any harder than before but just a lot smarter, adopting scientifically proven eating and training regimes.

As I got fitter and stronger, it resulted in the most powerful epiphany I've had in my journey to date. Until now, all of my effort and endeavours were dedicated to a very narrow and superficial element of fitness, i.e. body image.

While I recovered my self-esteem, it became strongly evident that my newfound level of fitness helped me excel in so many other aspects of my life. The feel-good hormones called endorphins released when you exercise meant I felt euphoric on a daily basis, which got me mentally prepared for the challenges ahead, especially at work. I also found myself sleeping a lot better and either getting sick less often or bouncing back a lot more quickly from bugs that, in the past, would have me grounded considerably longer.

Since then, I have been motivated to maintain and improve my fitness base for holistic reasons, i.e. healthy mind, body and spirit.

What was the hardest challenge you ever faced mentally and physically, and how did you get through it?

I recently unsuccessfully attempted to break the World Record for the most amount of push-ups in one hour. Funnily enough, I unofficially broke the record weekly for 8 months leading up to the official WR attempt. In hindsight, this clearly proved to be my undoing. Just like marathon runners don't run marathons every week for months and weeks before their event, I should have spared my joints by a less taxing preparation enabling me to perform at my best on the big day.

Ironically, the same wrist that broke down all those years back and resulted in my fitness journey came back to haunt me. Just like then, though, I plan to turn this negative into a positive from learning from my mistakes and giving it another crack in the not-too-distant future.

How did you manage to balance all the different areas of your life?
As soon as you make any aspect of your day-to-day life non-negotiable, whether it be eating, showering, and going to work, etc., then you just do it. Exercise and a healthy diet very much fall into that non-negotiable category for me. This helped to breed a level of habit, which made willpower redundant.

I constantly get, "Wow, I really admire your willpower", and my stock standard response is that I only required willpower for the first 3 to 4 weeks about 20 odd years ago when I embarked on this journey. Since then, it's become so habitual that it's become as natural and instinctive as breathing.

Did you have to make compromises?

I need to travel regularly for work, which means that my training regime and access to gyms is affected. I actually see this as an opportunity instead of a compromise, as I genuinely believe in the training philosophy of adaptation. Our bodies are very good at becoming more efficient (by adapting) and hence allowing less energy expenditure when it gets used to doing the same type of exercise and movements.

Adaptation explains why beginning exercisers are often sore after starting a new routine, but after doing the same exercise for weeks and months they have little, if any, muscle soreness. This reinforces the need to vary a workout routine if you want to see continued improvement. This is why I see travel now as an opportunity to vary my routine by doing different body weight types of exercises in my hotel room, which I don't ordinarily do.

Can you run me through your typical day in terms of work schedule, exercise, food intake, supplements etc.?

After aiming for a minimum of 6.5 hours sleep, my day begins at 5.30 am where I respond to emails from my US colleagues who are at the opposite end of the day.

I hydrate (but don't eat) then set off for an easy 3km run to my local gym where I do the following:

- 10-minute interval training on an elliptical trainer.

- 30 minutes weight-bearing activity (2 body parts per session) with minimal rests between sets.

- 10 minutes interval run on the treadmill (30 seconds sprint/recover intervals).

- Relatively hard 3km run home.

True to my adaptation philosophy, though, I try to change this up from time to time.

In terms of food and supplementation, the only exclusions are junk food and simple/white carbohydrates, e.g. refined table sugar and white bread, etc.

Most of my nutrition comes from whole foods, as I genuinely believe supplements are called supplements for a reason, i.e. that you should only supplement a well-rounded healthy diet and lifestyle. I do use natural whey protein supplements as a means of achieving the necessary level of protein my body requires, as you can only have so many eggs and chicken breasts!

Whilst the jury is still out on the need for vitamin and mineral supplementation, I do take a multi and Vitamin C as more of an insurance policy in case my daily food intake is insufficient and to ensure my immune system is as strong as it can be.

What's the one thing you wish you knew 20 years ago?
Knowledge is more important than willpower.

What advice, tips, and specific strategies would you give to corporate executives like you who are struggling with competing priorities?

Use corporate objective setting methods such as SMART goals.

"Contract" these SMART goals, i.e. tell people close to you so that you become more accountable.

Move heaven and earth to get through the first 3–4 weeks of your regimen because by then it's likely to become habitual and the only thing you know.

What drives you when the 'going gets tough'?

Having experienced that euphoric sense of achievement following prior triumphs gives you the motivation to push through pain and adversity.

How do you manage overseas travel – aeroplane food, conferences, conventions and meetings and still keep to your regime?

When I first started to travel for work, a healthy diet and lifestyle was more on the periphery of society, and hence it was more difficult to find healthy alternatives on planes and at conferences. There is absolutely no excuse today with healthy eating becoming more mainstream due to the growing demand. Most airlines have healthier options and conferences usually cater for specific dietary requests.

What's taken a lower priority in your life as a result of competing demands?

Vegetating in front of the television watching mind-numbing, inane programs.

This is the Beginning

– A Conclusion

"The beginning is the most important part of the work."

Plato

I hope you have enjoyed the journey so far.

I have given you the strategies and tools that you need to make the changes you want in your life, but if you take those tools and put them away, they will be useless.

You need to use those tools and implement those changes. Nobody can do that for you! You are the only person that can do that. You need to be so convinced of what the reason is as to *why* you want to do this.

Why is it that you want to be fit? You have picked up this book for a reason. You have a problem that needs to be solved and I have the solution.

That solution will only work if you make some conscious effort and do something about it. Your part of the deal is that you need to stay focused, keep aligned with your vision, your goals and your compelling outcomes.

There will be times when everything seems too difficult, and they are the times that really count. I was very fortunate to speak to the legendary Australian former world champion marathon runner Robert de Castella and I asked him what motivated him, what kept him going to do everything that he needed to do.

He said to me:

"It doesn't count when it's a beautiful sunny day and it's a perfect day for going for a run along the beach. That's not when it counts."

"It counts when its pitch dark outside, when it's raining, and everybody else is in bed and fast asleep. You get up and you go out … and it's dark, pouring rain and freezing cold. That's when it really counts."

Every time my alarm rang at 05:05 am in the morning, for a moment the thought of getting up and going to a cold, muddy oval to do my morning run felt too hard, as I felt the warmth of my doona which felt so good. The chatter would start in my head about all the reasons why I should stay in bed.

This is the Beginning – A Conclusion

"I need my sleep."

"I need a rest."

"I have a big day ahead of me."

"I worked so hard. I deserve to stay in bed for a bit longer."

"My legs hurt from yesterday's exercise session."

There were always so many excuses disguised as reasons as to why I should stay in bed, and then I would always hear Robert de Castella's voice in my head saying, "This is when it counts. This is when it counts."

I made sure that this was when it counted and I made the decision when it counted.

So, if I can leave you with anything, it's that. Make the choices that count, make the decisions that matter. It's not about doing it the easy way or doing whatever you feel like doing, or waiting until you 'feel' like exercising. Embrace that non-negotiable mindset. You just have to do it because this is when it really counts.

If you want to be healthy and enjoy your life, if you want to be there for your children and your grandchildren, and you want to reap the benefits and the successes of everything that you have worked so hard for, then you need to make the harder choices. You need to make the more difficult choices.

At this very moment, you are at a fork in the road of your life. There's a road that goes to the left and there's a road that goes to the right.

The road on the left is a downhill road and it's easy to go down the downhill road because it's what you have been doing for so long, coasting along with little effort, making easy choices.

But it's the path of misery. It's the path of not living your life on your terms. The path on the right goes uphill and it takes a little bit more effort to go on that road. It's the road of making the harder choices, but it's the path that takes you to that healthy successful future.

Once you are on that path, each step gets easier and easier. Every step that you take becomes an easier step than the step before. You can reap the rewards of everything that you have created up to this point in your life.

My request to you is to take the high road of success on the right. Leave the past behind and move forward to a compelling future that is waiting for you, because you know that you can do anything that you focus your mind on.

Surge forward. This is the day that you decide to reclaim your life.

Life is this wonderful, unique, experience and we need to make the most of every single moment.

This is the Beginning – A Conclusion

I hope this book has been of enormous value to you.

With all my love,

Helen.

HELEN MITAS

https://www.helenmitas.com/

Mindset Dominance

www.ingramcontent.com/pod-product-compliance
Lightning Source LLC
Chambersburg PA
CBHW071617080526
44588CB00010B/1168